Chickens
in your
Backyard

Chickens in your Backyard

A BEGINNER'S GUIDE

by
Rick and Gail Luttmann

Rodale Press, Inc.
Emmaus, Pa. 18049

Library of Congress Cataloging in Publication Data

Luttmann, Rick.
  Chickens in your backyard.

  Bibliography: p.
  Includes index.
  1. Poultry. I. Luttmann, Gail, joint author.
II. Title.
SF487.L968   636.5   76-14357
ISBN 0-87857-125-6   paperback

Illustrations by Sidney Quinn

Printed in the United States of America on acid-free ∞, recycled paper

Distributed in the book trade by St. Martin's Press

30   29   paperback

This book is respectfully dedicated to Humpty Dumpty—
our favorite egg.

Contents

We would like to thank our friend George Matson for helping us remember all of the questions beginners ask; our neighbor Gina Williams, who proved that a beginner could understand what we wrote; and Mom, who always said we ought to write a book.

0
Before the Beginning

There's little wonder that no one knows which came first, the chicken or the egg. Raising chickens is a continuous cyclical process, and the only way to describe it is to break into the cycle at an arbitrary point and call it the beginning. In organizing this book, we have chosen one place to start, but your immediate needs may require you to start somewhere else or to skip chapters of no importance to you right now. We've organized the material to make it easy to do this. We recommend, though, that everyone first read Chapter 1, "Words You Should Know," and refer back to it when the meaning of any special poultry term is unclear.

In raising chickens ourselves and in talking about it to others, our philosophy is that mindlessly following somebody else's list of rules is no substitute for a thorough understanding of the nature of chickens, the function of the equipment, and the purpose of the husbander's various activities. For one thing, a little initiative can save you a lot of money. There's no need to buy fancy expensive equipment when, with a little savvy, you can modify something you've got lying around the garage to suit your needs. (If you can cleverly improvise even once, you may save more than you spent on this book!) As long as the chickens' needs are met there's no one right way of doing things, though there are a lot of wrong ways. That's why our advice will usually be "You *could* do so-and-so" instead of "You *must.*"

For another thing, there is such a variety of reasons for raising chickens that we have to allow you a little flexibility. Maybe you want a couple of pet banties running in the backyard, or maybe you want your flock to supply meat and eggs for your family, or maybe you are mainly interested in winning first prize at the county fair. Your particular purpose will determine your perspective.

Finally, the better informed you are, the less likely you'll get gypped. More to the point, you won't go moaning around because you *thought* you'd been gypped when you hadn't. For example, you might complain that your new hens aren't laying. But if it's winter, chickens typically don't lay well (as you'll soon find out), and by midspring you'll be so sick of omelettes, quiches, and Denver sandwiches that you'll be begging the chickens to stop. We don't mean to imply that *no* used-chicken salesmen are crooks. To the contrary, there are always a few scoundrels around who take deliberate advantage of the unwary, while some dealers may be merely incompetent or innocently ignorant. But most chicken raisers are honest and helpful folks who want to share their experiences and their love of birds with you.

People who are just getting into raising chickens occasionally express the opinion to us that all the lavish care chicken raisers expend on their flocks seems unnatural and unnecessary, for surely chickens must have gotten along all right for thousands of years out there in the jungles all by themselves. But remember that chickens as we know them today have come a long way from their natural state, due to domestication and controlled breeding by man over the centuries to suit *his* needs. As a race we have made a Faustian bargain with the chickens, and we must now pay the price of having molded them to our needs by giving them the special care they have come to depend on and require. Chickens have simply been pampered for too long.

You must forgive us if we tend to anthropomorphize a little throughout this book, for we have come to think of chickens as our friends. Sadly, we must admit that they are among our least intelligent friends. But nature has given these creatures a generous measure of instinct by which they have managed to survive. Our function as husbanders of a flock is to work with and direct their instincts, adding our wit and wisdom to ensure

2

that they prosper and flourish. This book is a guide to enlightened intervention in the affairs of chickens.

It is a book for beginners—the ABC of Chickens, so to speak. Although we don't have a degree in Chickenology qualifying us to write a book, we are experts in beginner's mistakes, having made most of them ourselves! When we started raising chickens we looked everywhere for a good, clear, comprehensive, nontechnical, noncommercial book about raising a flock in the backyard. It didn't exist. So we wrote it, and here it is.

1
Words You Should Know

There are a number of words peculiar to the language of poultry raising. It is important to know and understand these words when talking to other people about chickens. This helps avoid confusion, especially if a word possesses a different or more precise meaning than it has in common usage. We hope that this section will be useful to you as a reference both when unfamiliar words come up in your conversations with other poultry people and when they occur later in the text. If some account seems incomplete here, remember that this is just a glossary and things will be developed more fully in the text.

A bunch of chickens is officially called a *flock*. "Chicken" means a kind of bird but does not tell you the sex of the bird. Adult female chickens are called *hens,* and adult males are called *roosters* or *cocks*. A male younger than one year is a *cockerel,* and a female under one year is a *pullet* (don't confuse this word with "poult," which is a baby turkey and has nothing to do with this book). A baby chicken of either sex is called a *chick*. A *capon* is a cock whose sex organs have been deactivated by some means. Any such process is *caponizing*. Capons have characteristics that are desirable for meat production.

Chickens venture forth during the daytime, but they always return to the same place to sleep at night. This habit is called *roosting,* and the place they return to is the *roost*. They like to sleep with their toes wrapped around something like a tree branch or ladder rung, referred to as a *perch*. Anytime a bird is sitting on such a thing, whether it is sleeping or not, it is said to be *perching*.

Chickens come in two sizes: large and *bantam* (also called *banty*). Banties are not a separate breed or species; they are simply small chickens.

Chickens, like horses and dogs, come in different breeds. *Purebreds* are those of one single breed sharing distinguishing characteristics that make them all alike; chickens of mixed breed, often of unknown ancestry, are called barnyard chickens (or *barnies*). There are also *hybrid-crosses* or *crossbreeds*, developed for certain outstanding characteristics and produced by always mating chickens of the same two different pure breeds. Chickens that are purebred will *breed true*, which means that offspring of a pair of chickens of the same breed will also be of the same breed and will more or less have the same characteristics. Barnies of indeterminate origin, and to a certain extent hybrids and crossbreeds, will have offspring with wild conglomerations of characteristics that can rarely be predicted accurately (but are often spectacular).

Pure breeds are grouped into different *classifications,* which usually tell the place of origin. Some classifications are Asiatic, American, and Mediterranean. New Hampshire Red is one of the breeds of chickens within the American classification, for example, and Leghorn is a breed within the Mediterranean classification. Breeds themselves are broken down into *varieties,* which tell more about the chicken. Brown Leghorn and White Leghorn are two varieties of the Leghorn breed. (Incidentally, Leghorn is pronounced LEG-ern.)

The *Standard* refers to the *Standard of Perfection,* a book published by the American Poultry Association, which describes the appearance of each breed and variety—color, weight, shape, feathering, etc. If you want to show your chickens at the fair, they should conform to the *Standard;* the extent to which they do determines the prizes they get. A standard-bred chicken is any one which appears in the *Standard of Perfection.* The book is fun to look through, even if you don't intend to show your chickens.

The word "standard" is sometimes used incorrectly to refer to large-sized chickens, as opposed to bantams. We once heard a confusing conversation centered around the statement, "Araucanas come in many sizes but there is no standard." Araucanas are a type of South American chicken, with a wide range of variation in their characteristics. The quoted statement means that Araucanas have not been accepted as a single well-defined breed by the *Standard of Perfection,* so there is as yet no accepted standard of color, size, and general body type. It doesn't mean that Araucanas don't come in the large size—they do, and in fact, they come in all sizes, from bantam on up. This confusion occurs because the word "standard" is often misused.

The polite word for chickens' excrement, or manure, is *droppings.* The polite word for the opening it comes out of is the *vent,* which also happens to be the opening the eggs come out of. Some of our friends find this appalling. We refer them to the Manufacturer. The eggs come along a different track, however, known as the *oviduct.* Just in front of the vent on the underside of the chicken are two sharp, pointed bones coming back from the breastbone. These are the *pubic bones,* and husbanders need to check them occasionally to see how well a hen is laying.

Chickens eat differently than we do. They don't have teeth or stomachs. When they eat, food goes directly into a little pouch at the base of their necks called a *crop,* which bulges after a meal. Eventually, food passes further inside to the *gizzard,* where it's ground up for digestion. The grinding agent, whatever it may be, is called *grit.* You'll have to purchase some at the feed store to give your chickens if they can't get it naturally in the form of pebbles. We are occasionally asked if this is the same product as grits sold in grocery stores. It isn't. The traditional chicken feed is called *scratch,* which consists of a mixture of various grains. Chickens are called *ground-fed* when they are not kept in cages and can find food by foraging.

There are a few miscellaneous parts of a chicken's anatomy you may hear about. The part of a chicken's leg from the foot to the first joint is known as the *shank.* It is usually naked and scaly, but in some breeds feathers grow all the way to the ground. *Spurs* are the sharp horny protrusions on a cock's shank which he uses to stab people he doesn't like. He also uses them in fights with other cocks. Their length and condition give you a rough idea of the cock's age. The superstructure on a chicken's head is called the *comb,* and the dangly things under the chin are *wattles.*

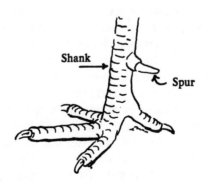

The words "mate" and "breed" are not quite synonymous. *Mating* refers to the forming of an allegiance between a male and a female, or sometimes a male and several females. Mated birds hang around together and have more social interaction with each other than with the rest of the flock. Wild birds tend to form strong matings, sometimes seasonal, sometimes for life. Chickens exhibit this behavior only mildly in that roosters usually try to gather harems of hens to supervise. These liaisons are easy for the keeper to rearrange or terminate (while those of, say, geese or mallard ducks are not). *Breeding* refers specifically to the performance of the sexual act. This word is also used in another sense—to refer to the genetic control exercised by a keeper to ensure offspring are produced only by certain pairs of birds that he chooses. It is very rude to confuse these two meanings of the word, especially when you are talking to a chicken breeder.

The chickens you own are sometimes called your *stock*. If you save certain chickens specifically for breeding, they are called your *breeding stock* or your *breeders*. If you have excellent specimens of chickens for show that would win prizes at exhibitions, they are called *show stock*. If you are careful about choosing which chickens you allow to breed with each other in order to exercise genetic control over the characteristics of their offspring, you are practicing *selective breeding*. Breeding chickens that are closely related is called *inbreeding*. When a chicken bears more resemblance to one of its distant ancestors than to its parents and other more immediate relatives, it is called a *throwback;* it is necessary to study the principles of genetics in order to understand why this anomaly happens.

An egg is described as *fertile* or *infertile* according to whether or not it is capable of producing a chick. Fertility depends on how recently a rooster has bred the hen that laid the egg and how vigorous the rooster is. When an egg is laid it has a slimy wet covering called the *bloom* that has eased the egg's passage through the oviduct. The bloom dries quickly into a thin, invisible membrane. A batch of eggs in a nest is called a *clutch*.

Eggs will hatch only if they have undergone a period (of

varying length, depending on the species of bird) called *incubation,* during which they are kept suitably warm and moist. In nature this is accomplished by a hen. Presumably hens do not know what they are doing or why they are doing it; they just take a notion to go off to a quiet corner and sit on a clutch of eggs. This kind of sitting is called *setting,* and a hen that is in the mood to do so is called *broody.* Calvin Coolidge once remarked that, in his native rural Vermont, whether a hen was sitting or setting wasn't considered as important as whether she was laying or lying.

If you don't want a hen to set, you have to *break* her *up,* which means discouraging her broodiness through various means. Some people say "bust up" because they think it sounds tough; but hens are not so easily intimidated. Don't worry that if you break up your hen her deepest primal urgings will go unconsummated. She'll forget all about it in a day or two. Assuming that you elect not to break her up or that she elects to ignore your attempts, one day a batch of chicks will *hatch* (they are never "born"). They make a hole in the eggshell through which they breathe while struggling to get out. Making the hole is called *pipping.* The batch of chicks is referred to as the hen's *brood.*

Incubation may be accomplished artificially in a device called an *incubator.* It may be large or small, simple or elaborate, but it must simulate the temperature and humidity underneath a setting hen. During incubation you may want to see what's going on inside the egg by shining a powerful light through it. This is called *candling,* although it is no longer done with a candle. The same process, known by the same name, may also be used to check eggs for cracked shells or internal blood spots when the eggs are going to be sold for eating.

It is nice to know a baby chick's sex as soon as possible. The process of sorting out the pullets and the cockerels is called *sexing* and is done by professional *sexers* employed by hatcheries, which are places that specialize in hatching chicks, usually breeds of commercial value. When you buy chicks you can get all pullets (for more money) or all cockerels (for less) — but

9

don't expect perfection, as even professionals are only about 95 percent accurate. You can also buy *straight-run* chicks, which means they have not been examined and sorted by sex and are mixed in natural proportions of about 50-50.

Chicks that are hatched without a hen are usually (but not necessarily) raised without a hen. They must be kept warm and safe in an enclosure called a *brooder* while they are growing up.

When chicks are hatched, they're covered with soft downy fluff rather than feathers. They begin to grow feathers immediately, however, and after they have a complete set of actual feathers they are said to be *feathered-out.* This means they can fly and keep warm, but it does not mean they have acquired their full adult plumage. *Plumage* refers generally to a bird's configuration of feathers in their different lengths, shapes, and colors. Once a year, usually in autumn, the feathers fall out and are renewed. This is called the *moult* (sometimes written *molt*). Fortunately, the process is gradual so the bird is seldom completely bare, though we've seen some come close.

Chicks sometimes *pick* each other, pulling each other's feathers out around the vent or head or other places. Older birds will also do this if too many are kept in too small a space or if they are bored. Sometimes picking goes on so extensively that it is called *cannibalism.* Chickens are definitely carnivorous and will devour each other if they take a mind to. They may also discover that eggs have good things to eat inside. Then you have an *egg-eating* problem on your hands, which can be difficult to eliminate.

Brooder floors and coop floors should be strewn with some absorbent material that is durable, does not pack easily, and permits quick evaporation. Such material is called *litter,* and it can be straw, pine needles, wood shavings, sawdust, rice hulls, or any number of things. If the litter in a brooder gets wet and messy, chicks might get *coccidiosis,* or *coccy* (COCK-see), a disease to which they're especially susceptible when young. Feeds for baby chicks often contain a disease-inhibiting agent called a *coccidiostat* that greatly reduces the danger of this disease.

Chickens like to *dust,* or thrash around in the dirt, raising a cloud of dust around their feathers to clean themselves and to kill body parasites. Chickens have a *pecking order* whereby they arrange themselves socially by rank. If this subject interests you, read Konrad Lorenz's fascinating book, *On Aggression.*

With this quick synopsis of the poultry world behind us, let's go into the details.

2
Protecting Your Chickens

Beginning chicken raisers often wonder if there is really a need for fencing in chickens. There are at least two good reasons for confining them. One is to protect your garden and other vegetation from them (we'll discuss this in the next chapter). The other is to protect the chickens from predators such as hawks, raccoons, skunks, weasels, cats, dogs, kids, and cars. We've heard many a sad tale of various poultry pets disappearing. The following accounts will serve as examples of what could happen if you leave your chickens exposed to the cruel and hungry world.

We frequently see hawks flying around our area and several times have managed to chase them away from our yard before they did any damage. But one year, before we put in a coop, we saw a hawk carry off our little black banty hen. We felt both sad and outraged to watch our pet disappear. Some of our friends with hawks living on their property are certain the big birds would never touch their chickens. Maybe they're right — but one swift and sudden swoop could cost them their favorite bird.

In earlier times, it was common to see chickens running loose, and in some areas you can still see them along the roads. But things are changing fast, and road traffic can be a real hazard. Since we started raising chickens, we've experienced rapid population growth in our area and the accompanying advent of fast and furious traffic on our road. When our chickens used to run loose in the yard, a mother hen would occasionally take her brood across the street to eat the bugs in the neighbor's petunias. One time an old farmer in overalls stopped his vintage car, sat with a big toothless grin on his face while he watched the chicks cross, and then drove on with a wave. Nowadays drivers with such patience and understanding are rare, and the traffic is so bad that we get nervous just crossing to the mailbox each day. So last year we built a proper coop with enclosed runs to protect our chickens.

Some people believe that if they raise their dogs and chickens together, the dogs will learn not to go after the chickens. One of our neighbors told us that his dog let little chicks play between his paws and take naps under his chin while he slept. He said the dog even kept track of the chickens, making sure they didn't go anyplace they weren't supposed to. If the dog saw the chickens scratching around in the garden, he would herd them back to their own area. We were so impressed that we went out and got ourselves a puppy that we could train to help us keep the chickens in line. We also thought he might protect the flock at night by keeping away midnight marauders, or at least alerting us to them by barking. All went well until he was about four months old. Then one day, when we went out to feed the chickens, we found half-a-dozen limp, recently killed fryers lined up in neat order. We called Puppy over and told him how upset we were and that he mustn't do it again. The dog seemed to understand and for a while didn't give us any more trouble. Then one day we saw him chasing the chickens again—but with his tail between his legs! Puppy knew it was wrong, but he couldn't help it.

We asked several area farmers what we should do, and the consensus was to tie one of the dead chickens around his neck and let it rot; the dog would be so disgusted he would never go after chickens again. Well, maybe we tied it on wrong or maybe the dog was just incorrigible, because he shook and shook that chicken until he got it around to where he could chew on it, and the next thing we knew he was happily munching the bones. So, it was either the chickens or the dog, and we settled for the chickens. What we hadn't known at the time was that some breeds of dogs apparently have a killer instinct, and our Samoyed was one of them. Perhaps had we gotten a different breed, the whole thing wouldn't have happened.

The neighbor whose experience had initially encouraged us didn't fare well with his dog either. The dog got a bit too frisky with the chicks one day and killed some of them by accident. He was so ashamed that he buried the bodies, and our neighbor didn't know what had happened to his chicks until a few days later when he came across the grave. But the dog eventually went on to more gruesome deeds. One night, early in spring, he broke out of his yard. He headed straight for our purebred bantams and chewed the legs off several of our hens through the bottoms of the cages. Yet he had never deliberately killed the chickens in his own yard. He was a canine Jekyll and Hyde.

As for kids—well, we have never understood what they get out of it, but some kids think it's fun to throw stones at roosting chickens or to chase birds around the yard until they're frantic with fright. Hopefully, if you let your kids help take care of the flock, they will develop a love and respect for birds. But the flock still might need protection from other children in the neighborhood.

We could write a whole book detailing the gruesome demise of various poultry pets of our friends and neighbors, but suffice it to say that a nice strong pen will keep your flock safe from most such fates.

3
Protecting Your Garden

Aside from keeping your chickens safe, another good reason for confining them is to protect the garden. You can make chickens your helpers if you work it right; but if given complete liberties in a garden, a flock of banties or even just a couple of large chickens can devastate the vegetables and flowers in no time. The first year we had both a garden and chickens, we made the mistake of planting the tomatoes right across the fence from the chicken yard, in full view of the flock. The sight of those luscious red tomatoes was just too much for the birds, and they always found a way, no matter how much wing clipping and fence patching we did, to get the ripe tomatoes just before we did. They were watching those tomatoes as closely as we were, and *they* got up earlier in the morning!

Chickens like to scratch around in the soil, and they don't care if the row of seedlings you just put out is in their way. They might uproot or bury the little plants, and very often they will dispatch them by gobbling them up as they go scratching along.

Nevertheless, chickens and gardens can go very well together, provided the chickens are properly managed and controlled. Allowing the chickens to scratch around in the garden when you are between crops is an ideal way to keep down insect infestations, and it also keeps your birds healthy. They may eat a lot of beneficial earthworms, but if the composition of your soil is good, the worm population will build back up in no time. Our chickens like to be on the scene when we till, and as soon as they hear the tiller they line up along the fence and start clucking excitedly. When we let them out, they follow along right behind the tiller.

Another trick for getting rid of garden pests is to lay boards in the garden plot, and then turn them over every few days and let the chickens in. You will get rid of a lot of slugs, earwigs, and sow bugs that munch on your garden at night and hide beneath the boards during the day.

You can allow a few chickens, especially bantams, into the garden once the plants have reached a good size. They might nibble at your crops a bit but will reduce the insect pest population at the same time. Keep an eye on them at first, lest your whole garden disappear in a single afternoon. The number of chickens you allow in the garden with no ill effect on the crops really depends a lot on what you plant and on the size of the garden plot. Some people keep banties in the garden all the time. Experiment—with caution!

Garden party.

4
The Coop

Before getting any chickens, you should decide where you're going to keep them. They will need a place to go at night where they will be safe from predatory animals, and dry and free from draft. It can be a very elementary shelter. When we first moved here, there was an old outhouse type structure for a coop, with a small door cut in the bottom for the chickens to go in and a perch for them to roost on. It was certainly simple and picturesque, and the chickens seemed to be healthy enough. The particular design you choose may have to be more elaborate if you want to raise several different breeds separately.

There are many types of coops. You might be able to remodel an existing building or even an old packing crate to suit your needs. One way to gather ideas is to take a look at the different kinds of coops other chicken raisers have built in the

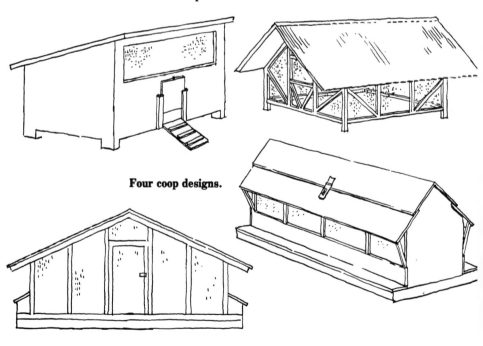

Four coop designs.

area. Most people will be delighted to show you around their coop. Regardless of the architectural design, however, there are certain features that are essential to all coops.

Your first consideration is the proper area of floor space. If you plan to raise large breeds at least four square feet will be needed for each bird, and bantams should have not less than two square feet each. Of course, if the chickens will be confined to the coop for a great part of the time, they will need more room; allow ten square feet for each large bird or six to eight square feet per bantam (and be especially careful to provide for plenty of sunlight and ventilation).

The height of the coop is mostly a matter of your own convenience. As long as the chickens have room to perch without bumping their heads, they really don't care if the coop is three feet or nine feet high. But you might. You will find that you frequently need to get into the coop to retrieve eggs laid in out-of-the-way places, to clean out the litter and manure that accumulate, and to catch chickens that always seem to know when they are at arm's-length-plus-two-inches. A coop can be small, as long as its opening is big enough for you to work through. We had one coop (quickly replaced) that was built something like an old-fashioned chest freezer, but with side walls just a little too tall to reach over with ease. We undoubtedly amused the neighbors no end with our stand-on-your-head, wave-your-feet-in-the-air egg-retrieving and chicken-catching act. And the coop was practically impossible to clean out. If you decide to build a fairly large coop, you will probably be much happier with it if you make it tall enough to walk into with comfort. There's nothing worse than cleaning out a dirty coop on a hot sweaty day with your head bent over because the coop is six inches shorter than you are.

The chickens should be able to roost on off-the-ground perches. A perch should be just thick enough for the chickens to get a good grip by curling their toes around it. Any two-inch-thick bar makes a good perch for large breeds, as long as the edges are rounded. For banties, you might use an old ladder or a broom handle firmly attached like the clothes bar in a closet.

19

Swinging perches, suspended with chains or baling wire, work very well for lightweight birds and can serve a dual purpose. Besides their use by the roosting flock at night, swinging perches also provide diversion for confined birds during the day. Even chickens get bored and like to play!

The perch should be installed far enough from the wall to allow the chickens to roost in comfort—at least one foot for banties and 18 inches for large breeds. Allow eight to ten inches per chicken along the perch for large breeds and about five inches per bantam.

A perch for banties can be higher off the ground than one for large chickens. In fact, banties prefer to roost way above ground, and some of ours even like to sleep in the rafters of the coop. Larger breeds prefer to roost at a more conservative height of two to three feet, probably because it's difficult for them to fly up very high.

Be sure that the chickens won't be roosting in a cross-draft. Chickens keep warm by ruffling up their feathers to create a thermal blanket that traps air warmed by their bodies. A draft blowing through the feathers will remove the layer of warm air, and protection against the cold night air will be lost. The coop design should provide for plenty of ventilation, though, to prevent the ammonia given off by the droppings from building up and to allow excess moisture to evaporate, thus keeping the environment more healthful both in summer and winter. There should be doors or windows that can be opened during the stifling summer heat. Chickens cannot take high temperatures and may die if it gets too hot.

Beneath the perch there should be a droppings pit, an enclosure that holds the droppings as they accumulate. This prevents the chickens from walking in the accumulation, thereby helping to keep the flock disease-free. The pit should be covered with a removable frame constructed of welded wire. If you plan to have baby chicks in the coop at any time, use 15- or 16-gauge wire in a 1-by-½-inch rectangular mesh. The welded wire may need support from beneath with a few one-by-two-inch cross-braces, depending on the dimensions of the

Roost and droppings pit with removable wire-mesh cover.

frame and on whether or not you intend to stand on it yourself.
If only older chickens are going to be walking on these frames,
you can use a larger mesh welded wire (1-by-1½-inches) that
will still hold the weight of the chickens without sagging, and a
few cross-braces as needed. You may find that chickens, especially larger breeds, prefer to roost on the pit cover rather than
on a perch.

The frames should not be permanently affixed but should
be easy to lift out so that the manure can be removed. If the
frames are difficult to take out, you'll be inclined to put off
cleaning beneath them. Remove the droppings before they
reach the top of the pit or when you begin to notice an odor.
Litter placed in the pit after each cleaning will help absorb
moisture and keep down the odor. Chicken manure is high in
nitrogen and is great for the garden, but use it only aged or
composted, as fresh manure is likely to burn your plants. The
litter will help by lessening the burning effect and will also
enrich your garden itself.

The coop roof should be made of a material that will not
collect and hold heat. We used to have a transparent green cor-
rugated plastic roof and found that it created an ovenlike effect
in the coop on hot, windless summer days. Metal roofing or ply-
wood covered with roofing paper work fine. A few small openings along the eaves allow moisture to escape and provide a little fresh air. You may want to insulate the roof if your area
experiences extremes of temperature during the year.

The floor can be quite simple if the coop is small—just make it one large droppings pit. In larger coops there will be areas, besides those beneath the perches, where you and/or the chickens will be walking; the floor should be one that will not collect and hold moisture, that is easy to clean, and that the chickens will not have trouble walking on. A dirt floor fulfills most of the essential demands and, of course, is inexpensive to install. If you want to put some effort and money into the project, a concrete floor is ideal, especially since it discourages the rodents that are invariably attracted to chicken coops. A wood floor, provided it is built at least one foot off the ground, will also discourage rodents, although it will be harder to clean than concrete. It is a good idea to throw litter on the floor wherever the chickens will be (as well as in the droppings pit) to absorb moisture and facilitate cleaning.

In planning access to your coop, bear in mind that you and the chickens will have different requirements. You could put in people-sized doors only and leave them open for the chickens, but you may find it desirable to provide additional small doors for the chickens to use. Our coop has private doors for the chickens. We cut 12-by-18-inch holes in the sides of the coop, about 12 inches off the ground. The cutout pieces became the doors, hinged at the bottom and latched at the top. When open, they rest diagonally on the ground and provide a ramp into the coop. A few pieces of wood nailed crosswise provide stairs.

If predators are a problem in your neighborhood, it's a good idea to build the doors so that they can be closed and latched shut at night after the chickens have gone to roost. The chickens will be protected from drafts, too. But don't forget to

Coop doors and ramps.

open them again next morning. Just how early you have to open them will depend on how crowded the coop is and on whether or not the chickens have access to food and water.

One of our friends had a chicken coop situated at the edge of a forest. His chickens went back to the coop each night, and he shut them in to protect them from forest creatures. One night he forgot. Nothing happened, so he foolishly decided he really didn't need to bother going out there after all. About a week later his chickens mysteriously disappeared in the night. There's an old saying that experience is the best teacher. When the tuition is high, it's worth learning the lesson through someone *else's* experience.

Some kind of nesting boxes will be needed in the coop. Supply one nest for every four hens. Nearly every publication on chickens lists some specific measurements for nests, but we find that as long as a hen isn't so crowded that she is uncomfortably cramped and likely to break eggs, and as long as she can get in and out with ease, almost any size will do. But be sure that the nest won't tip over if large hens stand on the edge. The chickens should be discouraged from roosting in the nests, as this causes the nest litter to soil rapidly. A piece of canvas or burlap hung as a curtain in front of the nests helps prevent roosting on the edge.

Some hens like a ground-level nest, but most prefer an elevated one—up to about three feet high. The arrangement we have seems to work very well for chickens of every size and is

Improvised nests of tomato flats and an apple crate.   **23**

inexpensive besides. We turn an apple crate on its side, forming two shelves, and put a tomato flat on each shelf. We put some straw in the flats to keep the eggs clean and to keep them from getting broken. Having the nests in a darkened, secluded area provides a desirable place for the hens to lay and minimizes the chances that egg eating will develop. A fake egg in each nest will encourage the hens to lay there.

A fairly elaborate way of building the nesting boxes (but well worth incorporating into a *new* coop) is to provide a way to gather the eggs from outside the coop. The hens go into the nests from inside the coop, but you need only lift an outside lid

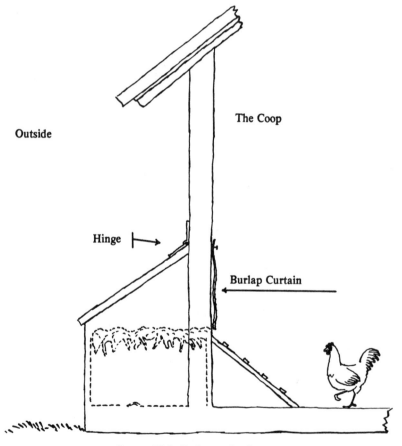

Coop with built-in nesting boxes.

to gather the eggs. This is really helpful if the coop is too small for you to get in and out of with ease or if you want to gather eggs without having to change (or clean) your shoes every time you go out.

Some people design coops with a special space in which to store feed and equipment so that it will be convenient and stay dry. If you want to include this feature in your plan, read Chapter 6, "Feeding Your Flock," to find out what you will need to have on hand so that you can provide space for an appropriate type and number of containers.

You might consider running electricity to your coop. This is especially desirable if it tends to get very cold in the winter, as chickens are prone to frostbitten combs and wattles; a few properly placed light bulbs kept burning at night will help keep the chickens warm and may prevent the drinking water from freezing. If lighting is available, it will be possible to stimulate laying during the winter (see Chapter 8, "Chickens for Eggs"); and with the modest heat available from light bulbs, chicks can be put into the coop at a younger age. Lighting will also be convenient if you ever need to go into the coop at night. However, electricity is a nuisance to install, and special arrangements must usually be made with the local power company and your county building inspector.

To be on the safe and sanitary side, it's a good idea to clean out and disinfect the coop at least twice a year. Remove the old litter and droppings, scrape away dried manure sticking to any surfaces, and scrub with disinfectant. A good disinfectant can be purchased at most feed stores. Dilute according to the directions on the can, and use a hard-bristle floor brush or a broom to brush it onto all surfaces. Be sure to get it into all cracks and crevices. A hose-attachment fruit tree sprayer is ideal for applying disinfectant, should you own one. Choose a warm dry day so that the coop will dry out soon after you're finished. It's a good idea to dry removable parts such as nests and dropping boards in the sunshine. When everything is clean and dry, apply the mite control of your choice (see the section on mites and lice in Chapter 14).

Now let's say you've gone through all that trouble of building a nice cozy chicken coop. You bring your new chickens home, and the first night you find them roosting in the trees. Birds that have been raised outside, especially banties, usually prefer to perch in the trees at night and do seem to be the healthier for it. However, for many reasons, we feel it's best to encourage them to sleep indoors. (If they get into the habit of sleeping outside they will continue to do so through rain, snow, wind, fire, flood, famine, and earthquake.)

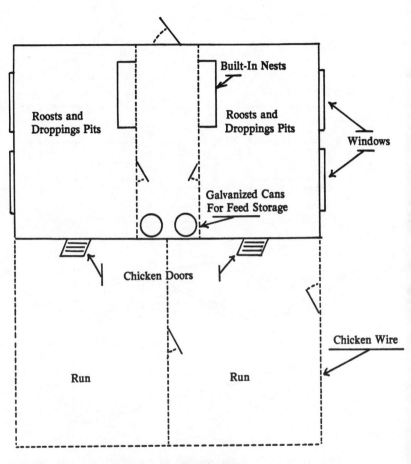

A coop design providing flexibility.

Two breeds could be kept separate to collect "pure" eggs for hatching; or, young chickens can be kept on one side, older ones on the other; or the door between the runs could be opened to provide maximum space for the entire flock. Dimensions of coop and runs will depend on the size of the flock.

27

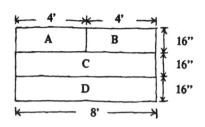

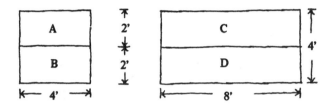

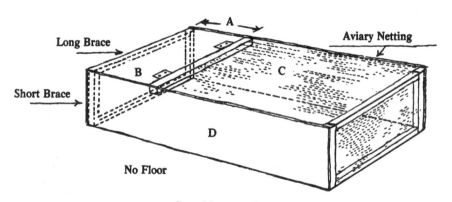

Portable ground pen.

This pen should be moved periodically to provide a new, clean floor with fresh greens. It is an excellent place for a mother hen to raise her chicks or for a brood of hand-raised chickens that are as yet too young to be housed with the older flock. It can also be used to separate a small group of birds for breeding purposes; or, placed some distance from the main coop, it will provide an isolation ward for sick chickens.

The best way to ensure that this problem doesn't arise at all is to release your new chickens inside the coop when you first bring them home, and to do so if possible at sundown. They will most likely return to the coop to roost every night, unless they have been used to sleeping outdoors at their former residence. If, the next evening, you find them thinking about an outside roost, discourage them by shooing them inside. If this proves difficult, the next day you might try luring them inside the coop by not feeding them until late, and then setting the feed inside the coop and shutting the door after they've gone in to eat. Especially stubborn chickens might have to be shut up in the coop for a couple of days.

After the birds have spent a few nights inside the coop, they will usually get the idea and go in of their own accord as the sun goes down. When you finally get them convinced, they will return to the coop even after a venturesome day in your garden. The old proverb about chickens always coming home to roost is quite literally true. All you have to do is to teach them where home is.

5
The Run

The larger and the greener the area in which chickens can frolic during the day, the better it is for them. An entire orchard, for instance, would be ideal. However, there are certain impracticalities in letting them roam anywhere they please: they may fall victim to various predators (see Chapter 2), they may destroy your garden (see Chapter 3), they may destroy your neighbor's garden (see a lawyer), and they will surely hide their eggs from you. Most people choose to confine their chickens to an enclosed yard or run. We don't recommend going to the extreme of keeping the chickens inside their coop all the time, if it can be avoided, because problems such as cannibalism and disease are more likely to develop and are more difficult to control when birds are so closely confined.

Chickens like fresh air and sunshine, but they know when they've had enough. If there is not sufficient sunny space, they will all try to get into a tiny patch of sunlight, and if the run is too exposed to sun, the chickens will crowd up in the shade on hot days. So make sure there is enough sun and shade to keep them all happy. If possible, the sun should reach all parts of the run at some time during the day so that the ground will have a chance to dry rapidly in wet weather.

Chickens love to dust themselves. They will lie on their sides and flap around in the dirt. This serves to keep them clean as well as to help kill some of the vermin that crawl on their bodies, so it is important that they have a place where they can dust. They seem to favor certain dusting spots over others, and after a while the run will have several deep holes in it. After a bath, they often like to bask in the sun in these holes, and they certainly can look very dead that way. Hence, if you see one ly-

Chickens dusting.

ing in a hole, all spread out and very still, check carefully before you panic.

Most chickens fly and all chickens wander about, so you need a fence around the run. Our fence is of one-inch mesh chicken wire, six feet high. (What we call chicken wire is sometimes called poultry netting.) The smaller the chickens, the taller the fence should be. Some banties can fly over a six-foot fence, but that height will stop most of them. Large chickens (except for some lightweight breeds like Leghorns) normally won't go over a three- to four-foot fence.

Usually it's unnecessary to cover the run, but if you have trouble keeping the chickens in, you could add a wire top. If that seems like too much trouble, you can also ground chickens by clipping their wings as described in the section on wing clipping in Chapter 14. Putting a wire top on the run is more work initially, but it solves other problems than keeping your birds from flying all over the neighborhood: if your flock is completely enclosed by the coop and the fencing, you won't have to worry about hawks or about closing up the coop every night, and wild birds won't be able to get in to eat the feed or transmit bird diseases and parasites to the chickens.

If you live in an area where wild animals such as rats, skunks, weasels, or raccoons might burrow into the run, it might be a good investment to put a wire bottom on as well. If the coop has a dirt floor, the bottom should extend under the coop too. This is done by digging up the dirt and laying down one-inch galvanized chicken wire. Place the wire deep enough that it won't interfere with dusting—about half a foot should do. Be sure to have a good overlap if you need more than one width to cover the area and join overlapping pieces with baling wire. Fasten the chicken wire around the edges to the inside of the coop and all around the edges of the fence. Replace the layer of dirt you removed and pack it down. (Of course this can be done in stages if necessary, covering a portion of the yard at a time.) Now the chickens will be completely safe from predators, and they won't be able to slip out under the fence by way of their dusting holes. Underground chicken wire tends to disintegrate after several years, so it will need to be replaced periodically. An expensive alternative, but one that will need less frequent replacement, is welded wire in a narrow gauge.

If you don't feel that you need to wire the whole bottom of the coop and yard, you might sink some one-by-six-inch rough redwood boards all around the edges of the fence with their tops just showing, and attach the fencing to them. This provides a good solid bottom for the fence. It also somewhat discourages both burrowing in and digging out.

Banty chicks can get through one-inch mesh chicken wire, so if you plan to have your bantam hens raise chicks in the coop, it's a good idea to put an edge of ½-inch mesh aviary netting around the bottom of the fence to a height of about 12 inches. It may be cute to see a concerned mother hen trying to call her unheeding chicks back into the yard, but you'll regret it if a cat or a hawk carries them off while the frantic mother flutters helplessly on the other side of the fence.

6
Feeding Your Flock

What you feed your chickens depends on three factors: their age and function; how much you're willing to spend on them; and what, if anything, they can obtain naturally.

PREPARED FEEDS

Since commercial chickens are almost always caged and are therefore totally dependent on the poultryman for adequate nutrition, the dietary requirements of poultry have been thoroughly researched. It has been found that chickens, like people, need a variety of foods in order to remain healthy and, like people, suffer severe nutritional disorders if certain constituents (including minute quantities of certain trace minerals) are missing from their diet.

Prepared chicken feeds are designed to provide a perfectly balanced diet for each type of flock. Most prepared feeds contain such ingredients as meat and bone scraps, blood meal, bone meal, fish meal, molasses, brewer's wastes, and ground grains and grain meals. They also contain minerals and vitamins that chickens are known to need. The protein content of these feeds is usually around 16 to 20 percent. The proportions of these components are varied somewhat by the manufacturers, depending on the special dietary requirements of the birds the feed is intended for. A complete line of special-purpose chicken feeds, including those for baby chicks, growing fryers, growing pullets, layers, and breeders, is available in most feed stores. The simplest and best feeding program for the backyard raiser is to give each group of birds precisely the special-purpose feed that is designed to meet their needs.

Many feed supply firms offer all-purpose feeds, one for

chicks and one for mature birds, along with their special-purpose line. Since it may be impractical for backyard raisers to feed each bird the most suitable special-purpose feed due to the small numbers of birds involved, the all-purpose feeds may be used as a compromise: all-purpose chick feed for birds up to five months, all-purpose flock maintenance feed for the older birds. Chickens will do adequately on such feeds—not quite as well as they would on feed mixed especially for them, of course, but the differences are minor and they most certainly will not suffer nutritional deficiencies.

Prepared feeds come in mash, crumble, and pellet forms. We find that chicks as well as grown chickens tend to waste the mash by spilling it on the ground. Therefore the crumble and pellet forms often prove to be more economical. Experiment to see whether your chickens prefer the crumbles or pellets. Pellets are too large for chicks so they should have crumbles.

Unless you have very few birds, we recommend against purchasing feed in small quantities because of the exorbitant price. Chicken feed is no longer cheap (even if it is still a metaphor for small-time financial doings), but when hundred-pound sacks are broken down and sold by the pound, the price can be outrageous. Prepared feed does go stale within a few weeks, however, so if your chickens won't go through a full sack within a short time, you might be forced to purchase your feed in small quantities.

Even for the backyard raiser who feeds his chickens a complete commercially prepared ration, there are many important, practical, and economical ways to supplement this ration such as letting the chickens forage over a pasture, feeding them kitchen scraps and garden wastes, and recycling eggshells. Regardless of what else may be made available to them, however, and regardless of whether they are caged, confined, or free, we strongly recommend the use of prepared feeds. For those who are inclined to mix or even grow their own feed, we discuss the specifics of proper chicken nutrition later in the chapter.

SCRATCH

The old-favorite chicken feed is a mixture of various whole grains with cracked corn. This feed, called scratch, goes over big with the chickens and has been an old farm standby since time immemorial. But it is not a complete dietary ration and makes a very unsatisfactory permanent menu. It's the equivalent of a human diet of pancakes for breakfast, lunch, and dinner. Caged chickens will be substantially undernourished if scratch is their sole feed, although they could get by solely on the single special preparation commercially designed for them. Chickens that are freer to roam about and forage in a pasture for part of their feed will have correspondingly better-balanced natural diets and correspondingly less need of the prepared feeds. For them, it would be appropriate to include a certain percentage of scratch in their ration, largely as a treat, but also in part because it is economical. Besides being cheaper, there is one additional advantage to scratch: it is composed largely of whole grains, so it isn't wasted if it falls to the ground and disappears in the dirt—since grain is seed it will sprout, and when the chickens eat the sprouts they will get more nutritional value than from the original grain.

Scratch mixtures with a high proportion of corn are not recommended. Some corn is fine, but as grains go, corn is lower in protein and higher in fat, and it tends to make the chickens obese. A *plump* bird is of course highly desirable. Plumpness results from full fleshing and is an excellent indicator of sparkling good health. But a fat hen doesn't lay well, a fat fryer on the dinner table is unappetizing, and a fat show bird is no more pleasing than a fat fashion model.

In cold weather it's a good idea to send the chickens to roost with a cropful of grain. The energy provided by digestion of the grain serves to keep them warm during the long winter nights. Putting the grain out just before sundown encourages them to fill up before going to roost.

FEED SUPPLEMENTS

Chickens must have access to grit in order for their digestive systems to function properly. Since chickens do not have teeth, the masticating function is performed by their gizzards. As a grinding agent, gizzards employ grit, which may simply be pebbles and other small hard indigestible objects that the chickens happen to eat. Grit gradually gets ground up along with the grain, so it must be continuously renewed. If chickens have a large area in which to roam, they usually get a sufficient supply of natural grit. For closely confined chickens, it's a good idea to purchase commercially prepared grit at a feed store and have a container of it available at all times for them to eat.

Laying hens need plenty of calcium to keep the eggshells nice and thick and to prevent them from eating their own eggs. An exclusive diet of lay mix presumably supplies a sufficient amount, and chickens having a wide range over which to forage generally get plenty. But if you're in doubt as to whether yours are getting enough calcium, you should make ground oyster shells available to them. Occasionally eggshells may be very thin or even absent (from time to time we've seen an egg with just the membrane covering it). This is a sure sign of a calcium deficiency. Egg eating may also be a sign that hens need more calcium, although other factors could be causing this problem (see the section on egg eating in Chapter 14).

A lot of people like to save up eggshells and feed them back to their chickens. This is an excellent way to recycle calcium, but the shells should be well mashed. Feeding chickens broken half shells could well turn them into egg eaters, even if they aren't calcium deficient, and this is a hard habit to cure. Their own shells alone do not provide a flock with sufficient calcium, and they should have an additional source unless they are running in a large area.

If range is available over which the chickens can roam, they will be able to find a lot of excellent, nourishing, and delicious food for themselves. Seeds and insects will provide them with protein, as well as the essential vitamins and trace minerals that are so vital to a chicken's health. The amount of nutriment that a pasture will provide varies somewhat with the nature of the vegetation. The younger and more tender the shoots, the more protein will be available from them. The older and tougher the vegetation, the more difficult it is to digest. Fibrous material may even become wadded up in the chicken's crop, blocking passage to the rest of the digestive system and making it impossible for the organ to function properly. The bird may eventually die of starvation. Granny had a catchy phrase to remind her of the proper type of vegetation to pasture chickens on: "The better for basket weaving, the worse for chicken feeding." Grass clippings (from lawns that have not been sprayed) are ideal for chickens, since lawns are generally mowed before the grass gets old and tough.

Chickens love fresh greens, salad scraps, weeds, and surplus or overripe fruit and vegetables from the garden. These are an important part of a feeding program for a backyard flock. Supplementing their diet with such things will help keep down your feed bill in general, but it is especially important if you are raising chickens for meat and eggs. If you raise them like commercial chickens, they will taste like commercial chickens and their eggs will taste like commercial eggs. Most people want something better than that for all their efforts, and often this is precisely why they are raising chickens. Our neighbor always tells us that our eggs are "eggier" than the store-bought variety, and she really likes their rich, orangey yolks.

If you don't have access to a lot of greens or weeds, sometimes yesterday's trimmings can be obtained from a fruit stand or the produce department of a grocery store. Produce people are usually very friendly and helpful and will sometimes even save things for you. (But now and then a grouch might threaten to call the sheriff on you, as happened once to us!) When you feed the chickens scraps, sort out anything that has begun to rot, as it might make the chickens sick.

We plant a number of chicken kale plants around our coop to provide the chickens with greens through the winter. This extra tall variety of kale is very easy to grow and flourishes during mild winter months, providing a good supply of fresh greens that chickens love. Because the kale is planted near the coop, the chickens can help themselves. But we have to provide some protection for the young seedlings, or the chickens would immediately eat the tender young plants right to the ground. After the plants grow tall and develop a thick stem, they are less likely to be destroyed by the chickens. If there is some leafy plant that grows well throughout the winter in your area, try it and see how your chickens like it. Chances are they'll relish any fresh greens they can get.

MIXING YOUR OWN FEED

Occasionally we're asked about the practicality of producing homegrown chicken feed for backyard flocks, especially by those who tend toward the organic. Although so-called natural feeds are sold by some feed stores, most grains have been sprayed with pesticides at some time.

We have found that the amount of feed that can be raised in a small plot is hardly worth the time and trouble needed to grow it and that there is very little monetary savings. In an effort to economize and to provide our flock with especially fine feeds, we have attempted to grow grains in our garden. Our first crop was a large patch of corn. After watering and cultivating the patch all summer, and cutting and drying the cobs in the fall, much to our dismay the chickens got into it without our knowledge and consent and gobbled it all down within a very short afternoon. Rather than providing a substantial supplement to their winter diet, it proved to be more of a treat—like a Christmas surprise.

We also tried growing a plot of oats one year. The crop grew well, with little trouble to us beyond occasional watering. But after the harvest had come we decided that the small amount of grain we were able to recover did not compensate us for the effort involved and for taking up a significant portion of the garden for an entire summer. It appears to us that growing a substantial supply of chicken feed in a small area is not practical. A large amount of land, the proper types of farm implements, and an adequate storage silo for the harvest would appear to be prerequisites for a feasible grow-your-own-feed project. We do find, however, that an essential portion of our flock's diet can be provided by scraps and weeds from our people-garden.

Some backyard flock owners have the facilities available to grow all or part of their poultry feed or may be able to obtain satisfactory constituents. For those of you in this situation, the following information is provided to help you formulate nutritious homemade rations for your birds.

A simple home-mixed ration might consist of:

- 65% grains, including at least two of these: barley, corn, milo, oats, wheat
- 7% alfalfa meal or ground hay
- 5% meat scraps, fish meal, or soybean meal (if necessary, substitute cooked soybeans for soybean meal; never feed raw soybeans to chickens as they contain toxins that inhibit growth)
- 13% dried peas or additional soybean meal
- 6% oyster shell or limestone
- 3% bone meal
- 1% trace mineral salt (obtainable in bulk from some feed stores)
- ½ pint cod-liver oil per 100 pounds feed

Naturally, with this feeding program you would want to provide the flock with grit, as mentioned earlier. Fresh greens, table scraps, and milk products should also be fed as available.

Whenever formulating a homegrown feed program, it is well to keep in mind that, as we mentioned earlier, different types of chickens have different dietary needs. For instance, birds raised for meat should be given feeds higher in protein than those raised for layers. Chicks also need the higher protein but should have less calcium. Birds raised for show will have to be fed according to breed, particular conditions, and your show schedule. When preparing mix-your-own feeds, the proportions of the components should be varied accordingly. For chicks and young birds, reduce the oyster shell from six to two percent, since too much calcium might damage their internal organs. Increase the soybean meal by seven percent to provide the extra protein for growth. Compensate for these changes by decreasing the grain by three percent.

You may want to provide homegrown grains as a dietary supplement to commercial feeds. In this case be sure to use a higher protein ration so that your flock won't fall short of your expectations due to protein deficiency. Mixed grains provide only about 8 to 10 percent protein, whereas layers require about 16 percent protein and growing birds need about 20 percent. You'll have to do some figuring when you use grains in conjunction with commercially prepared feeds.

Chickens in confinement will need to be fed more, and more carefully, than those on open range. You can tell if they're getting enough to eat—starving chickens act desperate when the feed is finally put out. You also have to guard more carefully against nutritional deficiencies and against obesity. These problems shouldn't arise if you use commercially prepared feeds. But if you mix your own feeds be cautious at first and watch for signs of nutritional deficiencies so that you can correct them right away. Some common nutritional problems are discussed in Chapter 14, "Advice and Solutions." Further information can be found in the book *Diseases of Poultry*, which contains an extensive discussion of dietary needs of chickens and gives detailed descriptions of nutritional deficiencies. *The Merck Veterinary Manual* also contains a section on poultry nutrition. (These publications are listed in the Appendix.)

HOW MUCH AND HOW OFTEN?

To give you some idea how much a chicken will eat and what your feed requirements would be for a whole year, figure that an average bantam in confinement may consume 40 to 50 pounds of feed annually while a large chicken might eat twice that. The exact amount, of course, depends on many factors, including breed, sex, temperament, and climate.

We like to leave a little something for the chickens to munch on all the time. They won't eat more than they need and so should be allowed to eat as much as they want. If encouraged to eat a lot, hens will often lay better, fryers will grow meatier faster, and show birds will remain in fine and healthy condition. Having tasty morsels to peck at all day also keeps the chickens from getting bored. But although feed should be continuously available, it is wise to feed them each day rather than to put a lot of feed out every few days. For one thing, it gives the chickens something to look forward to—they seem glad when we pay them a bit of attention and will usually eat what we just put out even if the same thing was already there for them. For another thing, it gives *us* something to look forward to, as it's a marvelous excuse to spend some time out with the flock. Besides, and more practically, it's a good idea to look around each day to make sure everything is okay.

Incidentally, just because chickens get up at the crack of dawn doesn't mean you have to get up that early just to feed them! Our friends always assume we must be early risers because we have chickens, and consider themselves at liberty to phone us at uncivilized hours of the early morning. But we just make sure there's some feed out at sundown so the chickens can breakfast while we're still in bed (and we hide the telephone under a cushion till we're ready to answer it).

FACILITIES

Feed can be stored in large plastic or galvanized garbage cans with lids to keep it from getting wet and moldy. Moldy feed should never be given to the chickens. These containers also eliminate the problem of rodents chewing holes in the sacks and robbing your grain.

Using feed troughs is more sanitary and economical than just throwing the feed on the ground. Look in farm catalogs and check with friends who have chickens to see what the different types of feeders are like, and then decide which would best fit your own needs. Many troughs have a wire guard to prevent the chickens from roosting over the feed, which is important because droppings in the feed promote disease. Droppings can also be kept out of the feed by attaching a narrow feeder directly to the wall so that the chickens don't have room

Compartmented trough, offering grits, shell, mash, grain, and greens.

to roost on it. A trough guard of some sort also keeps the chickens from scratching the feed out and wasting it and keeps them from dusting in the feed and spreading it all around the coop. It seems that no matter how much room the chickens have to dust outside, there are always a few that will dust in the feed if they can get away with it. Filling the trough too full also causes expensive waste of feed. Filling a trough only half-full is not unreasonable, and for caged flocks with shallow feeders, one-third full would be even better. Adjusting the trough to the height of the chickens' backs reduces the waste they otherwise cause by flicking the feed out while eating. The trough should be protected from rain, so either put it inside the coop or build a little roof over it. Don't attach the trough by any permanent means as it should be emptied and cleaned out regularly.

Chickens don't like stale feed and would rather starve than eat it. It's best anyway that they don't eat it. Once a week you should clean out the feed troughs and dispose of any residue in order to keep the feed fresh.

Feed troughs.

Any feed left in the open is fair game for wild birds, and the cost of feeding them can really add up when the feed bill comes in. However, in case it is impossible for you to exclude wild birds, there are some compensating advantages. For instance, as long as our wild birds are able to get plenty of grain, we find we lose a lot fewer cherries from our trees than do most of our friends without chickens. Also, the wild birds are just nice to have around, and some people go to a lot of trouble and expense to attract them.

At night, furry little critters may burrow up under the trough to eat the feed. A wire or concrete bottom on the coop would discourage this, as discussed in Chapter 4, "The Coop."

WATER

People sometimes tend to overlook the water supply. Plenty of fresh clean water must be available for chickens at all times. This cannot be overemphasized. They must have water with their feed to be able to digest it properly. A chicken is more than 50 percent water, and a large chicken will drink from one to two cups per day, depending on the weather. They cannot drink much at once so they must drink frequently. Furthermore, eggs are 65 percent water, and a hen that is unable to get enough water will be unable to lay properly. Even if she is deprived of water for only a short time, her laying may be seriously impaired.

Puddles of stagnant water from rain, leaky waterers, or whatever, are an ideal breeding medium for harmful bacteria and other disease-causing organisms and tend to become fouled by the chickens' excrement. Even if fresh clean water is available, puddles should be eliminated so the chickens do not have access to them. The birds themselves are not at all choosey about where they get their water, and therefore the quality of their water supply is only as good as the poorest available.

Avoid selecting waterers that tip easily; otherwise, the water must be replaced frequently, and a wet floor provides a good culture for germs. If chickens walk in the water they may get droppings in it and thereby cause diseases to spread. We strongly recommend automatic watering devices, even for only

One type of automatic waterer.

a few birds. During the hot weather, it can be quite a chore to go out several times a day to make sure the chickens have adequate water. Small automatic waterers are available for reasonable prices. They are easy to install on accessible faucets or with a length of inexpensive plastic pipe. Once the waterers are installed you can forget about them, except to clean them periodically to prevent algae from growing and to see that no dirt has gotten in to stop the flow.

If you live in an area that freezes in the winter, don't use plastic pipe, as it tends to burst easily when frozen. You might want to make some provisions for warming the drinking water because cold water is not good for the chickens. Besides, it's a nuisance to have to keep dumping out the ice and supplying fresh water. The pipes to the automatic waterer should be buried below the frost line, and the water bowl should be located inside the coop. If there is electricity in the coop, a light bulb over the water will help keep the water relatively warm. Also, small electric tapes are made to wrap around exposed water pipes and keep them from freezing.

It's no fun having chickens if they are a big pain. The amount of care they actually require, however, is minimal *if* you get properly set up and work out a daily routine of feeding and watering. You will find that using the proper types of equipment, designed to suit your needs, will go a long way toward simplifying your chores as a poultry husbander. A well-thought-out feeding program for your birds will assure a bountiful supply of meat, eggs, and baby chicks, and a healthy contented flock will bring you much satisfaction.

7
Roosters

We are asked so many questions about roosters that we feel they rate a chapter of their own. One of the questions we hear most often is "Do I need a rooster?" Well, unless you want fertile eggs, you really don't. The rooster has nothing whatever to do with whether the hen lays eggs or not. Furthermore, not even a chicken psychologist can say for sure if a rooster keeps the hens happy. It seems to us, actually, that hens are more relaxed without a rooster around to harass them. Let's face it, roosters are the original male chauvinist pigs! The common use of the word "cocky" reflects how outrageous their behavior is. However, roosters are half the fun of having chickens, and it is interesting to watch the full spectrum of social interaction in an integrated flock.

Listening to a cock talking to his hens is an enchanting experience. If he finds a tasty morsel crawling along the ground, he may pick it up and throw it down several times to make sure the hens see it, and cluck excitedly for them to come and share it with him. The sound he makes is the same as mother hens make to call their chicks, and it is clearly an important word in Chicken Talk. Sometimes, however, a cock will turn this to his own advantage, fraudulently enticing a hen to him with the same sound for less-than-honorable purposes.

A rooster does a dance number for hens that turn him on, a little vaudeville routine in which he skitters sideways and opens his wing feathers downward like Japanese fans—the chicken version of the strut that is found in many bird species. Peacocks are probably the most famous strutters, and of course everyone knows about Tom turkeys parading around all puffed up and proud. You can occasionally see wild birds going through their courting dances. In Germany and Austria there is a folk dance that mimics this bird ritual! It's called *Schuhplattler,* or shoe-slapping, and it is an imitation of the springtime antics of the male Austrian auerhahn, a grouselike bird that beats its wings loudly and rhythmically against its body and on the ground.

It is generally accepted that chickens don't mate as do some other species of birds. However, certain hens and cocks do have preferences for each other, always sharing their goodies and clucking endearments to one another throughout the day.

Dancing rooster.

The rooster will protect his flock, occasionally attacking when he thinks a member of his harem is being harmed. We've been threatened now and then by a normally friendly rooster when a hen we were carrying set up a squawk. This can be a real advantage in discouraging predators though, especially when you have a setting hen whose primary concern is protecting her eggs. The cock will in turn protect the hen. There was an article in the papers a while ago about an unsuspecting eagle that marched into a coop looking for a chicken dinner and was beaten to a bloody pulp by the rooster in charge.

It is entirely unfair that the word chicken has become synonymous in our language with coward. Admittedly, chickens have a well-developed sense of *discretion* about when to run. But more than once we've seen roosters put their lives on the line to protect their community. That's bordering on heroism and is more than some people are capable of.

Roosters are always on the lookout for hawks and will sound an alarm whenever they see one—or anything vaguely similar, like a biplane or a butterfly. They're very suspicious. Or paranoid. Or alarmist. But the rest of the flock all take it seriously: the other cocks immediately join the Chicken Little Falling Sky Chorus, and the hens and chicks all dive for cover. People can easily identify the hawk alarm, because remarkably enough, it's in English! The cry sounds exactly like a drawn-out "Hawk!"

Incidentally, it is rare that a rooster will attack a person, even with provocation, especially the person he belongs to and sees every day. Once in a while a cranky cock will have a mean streak, but generally there is no reason to be afraid of roosters. If you tend to be afraid of them anyway, do not assume that the larger ones are invariably the most fierce. Quite to the contrary, a feisty little banty cock can be formidable while roosters of larger breeds are often more mellow. In any case, roosters ordinarily reserve their rancor for each other.

Should you decide to have roosters, the next question is likely to be "How many should I get?" If fertile eggs are your main purpose in having cocks, then you need to find out about the rooster-to-hen fertility ratio for your breed. According to commercial experience, a young cock may fertilize eggs of 10 to 20 hens, depending on the breed, while an older fellow can handle only half that number. But since some cocks may tend to have certain favorites among the hens, all eggs still may not get fertilized, even if you do have a good rooster-to-hen ratio. And you never know which eggs are fertile and which aren't until you've set them to hatch for about a week, and by then the infertile ones are no longer good for eating. So, since roosters are very pretty anyway, it doesn't hurt to have a few extra if you don't mind feeding them.

Whatever your purposes, it wouldn't be wise to have more cocks than hens running in the same pen. For one thing, the roosters will do more laying than the hens, and the poor hens will be run ragged! For another, the cocks will fight more among themselves if there is more competition among them, and it could happen that they are so busy fighting each other that *no* eggs will get fertilized. A curious thing happens, though, if all the hens are removed from the pen—fighting among the cocks will cease almost entirely.

Even a reasonable number of cocks will fight occasionally. If you bring a new rooster into the yard, there will be a fight between him and all cocks-in-residence to determine the new pecking order. Unless the new rooster is particularly strong, the established cock will generally win. The fighting should subside once the new cock has found his place. When roosters are reunited after a separation, they may fight even though they formerly coexisted peacefully.

A rooster's place in the pecking order is dependent far more on his age than on his size and vigor. Fights are mostly bravado and strategy, and the outcomes are largely determined by psychology and experience. Fights between cocks already living together usually occur only when a young upstart challenges one of his elders. The older cock will usually win un-less he is quite old and his authority is waning. But if the younger cock is persistent, he will probably win in time.

So, fighting is normal and not much to worry about. Usually

the roosters will settle things for themselves and stop fighting before mortal wounds are inflicted. But if you are concerned about putting unacquainted cocks together, you might keep them on opposite sides of a fence or in adjacent cages for a while. This sometimes reduces chances of major bouts by allowing them to get used to each other gradually; when they are finally put together, their differences will hopefully be settled with a minor skirmish. Another trick that sometimes helps is to bring a new hen into the flock along with the new cock. If she is from his former flock, he will tend to stay with her, and the cocks already in the yard probably won't consider him to be as much of a threat.

Most fighting is not very serious. Not that the roosters think they're playing—they take it very seriously. But *we* don't take it seriously because fights seldom last long and rarely injure the combatants. This does not apply to battles over the very top position, which thankfully happen infrequently. These can rage on all day and may even result in the death or mauling of one of the contestants. If the cocks are drawing a lot of blood or are gashing each other with their spurs, they should be separated. If two cocks fight perpetually and inflict serious injuries on each other, one may have to be permanently removed from the flock. And if a cock has been weakened because of old age, injury, or disease, it's best to remove him before he is seriously injured by the younger, more vigorous cocks.

Incidentally, hens sometimes fight with the younger and weaker cocks or with each other. This is never serious, to our knowledge, and their big show of bluff is often amusing.

The most characteristic thing about roosters is their crow. Nearly everyone has an opinion about it, too. Some people refuse to have a cock around because they feel it disturbs the peace. Others insist on having one, and their only chicken will be a cock who'll wake them in the morning. A fellow we know named his rooster Reality because of his alarm-clock function.

For some people, hearing a cock crow in the morning is a pleasant experience. An old fellow stopped by one day to see if we had any spare roosters. We took him out to the coop and he listened intently until a rooster crowed. With a gleam in his eye and a grin on his face he pointed to the crowing bird. *"That's the one I want,"* he said, and scuttled off clutching his prize. That rooster was his only chicken—his bit of country life.

In some places it is illegal to have roosters precisely because they are so noisy, and the neighborhood's peace might be offended. If you're in doubt as to your zoning status, call the county zoning office to find out exactly what restrictions are enforced in your area. There was an item in the Pacific Poultry Breeders' Association newsletter recently about the hassle a member was having with the city council over his crowing roosters. When asked if there wasn't some way to keep the cocks from crowing, he replied, "Well, there *is* one operation that will prevent them from crowing . . . but unfortunately it also prevents them from breathing."

Actually, it is possible to have a rooster's "crower" surgically removed, but most veterinarians don't know much about it and won't attempt it. You would have to go to a specialist, and even then it would be very expensive and, except in extraordinary circumstances, not worth it.

It's a myth that roosters crow only at sunup. The truth is they crow anytime they feel like it. The only thing that can be said with certainty is that they sure do crow in the morning. But they continue to crow intermittently throughout the day and sometimes even at night. When they crow in the dark of the night, it's usually because of some outside stimulation. This could be from a light shining on or near them—say the headlights of a passing car, the back porch light you forgot to turn off, or a burglar's flashlight. They might also crow if they're disturbed by something or somebody moving in the coop, if they hear a loud noise, or if they hear another rooster crowing in the distance. One cock who's awakened by a passing car can get every cock in the neighborhood crowing. Usually it doesn't last long, and they all soon go back to sleep. When we first had chickens we would wake up when the roosters crowed at night, but now it's just become part of the normal night sounds and doesn't disturb us a bit, unless one has gotten loose and is perched on the bedroom windowsill when the sun rises.

8
Chickens for Eggs

Pullets will generally start laying when they are about six months old. Those hatched very early in the spring will sometimes lay in the fall, but it has been our experience that pullets reaching maturity during cold weather usually won't lay until it warms up again. Some experts say that hens are at their peak from one to two years of age and that a four- or five-year-old chicken is "old." But we find that we can still expect to get plenty of eggs to about four years, and we know of hens as old as nine years that are still laying. Nevertheless, you must expect fewer eggs as the hens get older and lower virility as the cocks get older. It's a good idea to raise a few young hens each year to prevent sudden decline of laying by your flock, and if economy is important, you should cull your flock periodically. This means checking hens for signs of good laying habits and eliminating those that appear to be lazy. A laying hen can be identified by her soft, deep abdomen; large, moist vent; and pubic bones that are wide apart. For each given breed, the hens with the larger, brighter combs are usually the better layers. If your purpose in raising chickens is economical egg production, you may want to follow commercial practices to a great extent. Information on the application of commercial methods to small flock raising can usually be obtained from local cooperative extension service offices.

We are often asked exactly how long a chicken can be expected to live. We have had no success in finding out since most authorities are more concerned with how long they're profitable. Chickens rarely die of old age. Most backyard birds are dispatched by unnatural causes such as predators, disease, culling, being eaten for dinner, or sold to a little old lady from Cucamunga and never heard from again.

Depending on what breed you have, you can expect to get an egg every day or two from each hen. Commercial hens were developed especially for egg production, so they usually lay better than others. A discussion of types of chickens to raise for eggs appears in Chapter 15, "Starting Your Flock."

Hens stop laying during the moult in autumn and then usually take a rest through the colder weather. Like autumn leaves, their combs lose their lustre and remain dull and shrunken during the nonlaying period. When the hens are ready to lay again in spring, the vivid color will return to their combs. A few hens may start laying right after the moult and continue to lay throughout the winter months; so, depending on the breed you choose, the weather, their diet, and the size of your flock, you might get some eggs most of the year.

If such fluctuations in egg laying can be expected from backyard chickens, you may wonder why eggs are available in markets year-round. Well, commercial producers use only hens bred specifically for egg laying, and they regulate the temperature and lighting in their hen houses to ensure optimum production. Naturally (or unnaturally), this tends to wear the hens out earlier in their lives, and they have to be replaced often; a commercial producer usually won't keep any one flock of hens for more than a year.

One of the reasons backyard hens don't lay as well during the winter is that the days are shorter. If you have electricity in your coop, you might burn lights for a few hours in the evening or early morning during the winter (as the commercial eggeries do) to simulate the 14 to 16 hours of sunlight of summer days and encourage your hens to continue laying. To save you the trouble of going out to turn the lights on and off each night, you might want to connect them to an automatic timing device (sold in department stores, and used to discourage burglars while people are on vacation).

Hens will generally lay their eggs in the nesting boxes provided for them, but occasionally they need the encouragement of fake eggs in the boxes. Fake eggs can be purchased at some farm supply stores, department stores, and import shops. Golf balls work fine as fake eggs too. Our first dummy egg was a white stone egg that we got for a joke one Christmas. It looks so real that when guests help us collect eggs, they invariably make some puzzled comment about "that awfully heavy egg." A rat once stole the fake egg out of a nest and must have had a time trying to crack it open down in its tunnel. A few days later it indignantly rolled the stone egg back out.

We found a store that had stone eggs of all colors and had fun picking out some wild ones to plant in the nests. The chickens seem totally oblivious to the colors so long as the egg is round and feels good. The theory behind using fake eggs is that when a hen sees eggs already in the nest, she will decide that it must be a safe place for eggs and deposit hers alongside.

Hens lay eggs in the oddest places. A hen's first egg, which

may be quite tiny, will often be laid on the ground wherever she happens to be standing when the urge strikes. It seems to catch her by surprise, and she doesn't quite know what's happening. But after the first one, she usually gets the idea and looks for a nest next time. Banties are especially fond of hiding their eggs. If you think you aren't getting all the eggs you should, look around for some hiding place—under a bush, behind the nesting boxes, or in the hollow trunk of a tree. If you have hens that like to play this kind of game, it would be a good idea to leave a fake egg in place of the eggs you take. Otherwise, the hen may decide to look for another place to lay that may be even harder for you to find. Since as far as we know chickens can't count (although some birds can), one fake egg will be enough: it would never occur to your hen that today there is only one egg where yesterday she had a whole bunch of them saved up.

Sometimes a banty hen will fly over the fence to lay her eggs in the bushes or weeds and then fly back into the coop area. We've found piles of eggs in places where we hadn't even known chickens had been. A hen will occasionally disappear altogether and, just about the time we think we've lost her, she'll come strutting back with a brood of little chicks following behind.

It's a good idea to collect eggs two or three times a day. There is usually a laying pattern, so after you've had your flock for a while you will know when they are likely to lay. Frequent collecting of the eggs keeps them from getting broken by other hens coming into the nest to lay or by chickens scratching around in the nesting litter. It also keeps them from being chilled or overheated during weather extremes and helps prevent egg eating from getting started. Predators are often attracted to the nests if the eggs remain in them overnight. If wild birds can get into the nesting boxes they may peck holes in the eggs, but they usually won't go into the coop to get at them.

Egg size depends on the breed of your hens. Large breeds lay bigger eggs than bantams, and some large breeds lay bigger eggs than others. A pullet's eggs will be smaller than a hen's, and small eggs are sometimes laid during summer hot spells.

Besides coming in a range of sizes, eggs also come in an assortment of colors, varying from white to a reddish brown. Usually one breed will lay one color, but there may be some variation. The only difference is in the color of the shell—the nutritional value of the contents is the same. Some hens (Auracana, or Easter Egg Chickens) even lay green or blue eggs. A friend of ours says he once had a hen that laid pink eggs with purple spots! It is popularly believed that colored eggs are higher in protein and lower in cholesterol, but to date this has not been scientifically substantiated. In fact, there is some recent evidence that the very opposite is true.

Incidentally, it is also commonly thought that fertile eggs have higher nutritive value than infertile eggs, and some people feel that they provide a more balanced diet. This, too, has not been proven. It is known that because the life factor is absent in infertile eggs, they do keep longer than fertile ones. This is really the chief difference to the consumer between fertile and infertile eggs, but it is not as significant today as it was in the days before the widespread use of refrigeration. Fertile eggs may start to develop an embryo if they are not refrigerated. In some parts of the world, eggs containing partially developed embryos are considered a delicacy (although this practice generated theological controversy over whether such eggs could be eaten on Friday). Most Americans would find such partially developed eggs unappetizing.

It's not impossible to tell whether or not an egg is fertile just by looking at it, but it's also not the casual matter some people assume. All eggs have a small white lump on the yolk called the blastoderm, which usually can be seen when the egg is cracked into a pan. People sometimes mistake this for a little chick beginning to develop. We have a friend whose aunt won't eat an egg when this lump is clearly visible, because she knows "what that hen has been up to." Actually, this *is* where fertilization takes place, but the lump is there whether the egg is fertile or not. With a close examination of the blastoderm you can distinguish between a fertile and an infertile egg. If the blastoderm is irregular and disorganized, and appears entirely opaque, then the egg was not fertilized. If it is neat and rounded with a small translucent eye in the center, you are looking at the very tiniest of baby chickens!

If nesting litter is kept clean and nests are not used for roosting, eggs should remain clean. Unless absolutely necessary, avoid washing eggs. A freshly laid egg is coated with a moist outer membrane—you may see it if you happen by at the right time. This coating, or bloom, dries right away, forming a barrier that retards moisture loss and prevents bacteria from entering the egg. The bloom is removed when an egg is washed, and the egg's keeping ability is thereby greatly reduced. This is of concern either if you want to hatch the egg or if you store it for consumption. Should an egg become soiled, try to brush or scrape the dirt off. If it does require washing, use it right away. There are those who don't mind cooking with dirty eggs, but we don't care for manure omelets and prefer to wash them when we feel it's necessary.

Some people like to candle their eggs in order to detect blood spots or cracked shells. The blood spots come from minor hemorrhages that occur along the hen's oviduct. Candling is important if the eggs are to be sold, although the spots are quite common and harmless. The only reason for discarding eggs with spots is aesthetic: that is, some folks are finicky. (Ideas for candling devices are described in Chapter 10 in the section on candling.) An egg may occasionally have blood streaks on the outside of the shell, but this need rarely be cause for concern.

Put eggs for consumption into the refrigerator as soon as possible after collecting them. They will keep for two weeks or more, but as they get older the white loses its firmness and the yolk may break when the egg is cracked. You can usually tell how fresh an egg is by how much it spreads when it's cracked into a frying pan. The fresher the egg, the more congealed the white will be and the more the yolk will stand up. Because these qualities also depend on the chicken's heredity and diet, they don't invariably indicate freshness.

Moisture evaporates from an egg with time, so an older egg will have a larger air cell than a fresh egg. The cell can be examined by candling or it can be measured indirectly by immersing the egg in water. When we were guests at a wilderness camp on Kodiak Island in Alaska, our host tested sea gull eggs by putting them in a bucket of water. The ones that sank, we ate for breakfast.

We have found that very fresh eggs are difficult to peel when hard boiled, but if they are boiled after the air cell has expanded over a few days the shells come off more easily. This is one case where freshness is not necessarily a virtue.

Freezing eggs is a good way to handle the summer egg surplus and provide for the winter shortage at the same time. Properly frozen eggs will be very much like fresh ones in appearance, flavor, and nutritional value. Eggs should be frozen only if perfectly fresh, and can then be stored in the freezer for nine months to a year at 0° F. or lower. Eggs to be frozen should be removed from their shells, for otherwise the shells may burst when the contents expand. One way to prepare eggs for freezing is to scramble them and add one teaspoon of honey or half a teaspoon of salt for each cup of eggs, to keep the yolks from getting pasty; then, pour the eggs into ice cube trays. The frozen cubes can be removed from the trays, stored in plastic bags, and thawed as needed. Thawed eggs should be used within 24 hours. Though eggs vary in size, for recipe purposes one egg is roughly equal to one cube or about three tablespoons. If desired, the yolks and whites can be separated before freezing; while salt or honey must be added to the yolks so they won't get gummy, the whites will be okay without any treatment. One egg equals one tablespoon of yolk and two tablespoons of white.

Fresh or frozen, the eggs from your backyard flock will provide you with ample resources for such exotic culinary treats as eggs Benedict, eggnog, custards, hollandaise sauce, and homemade mayonnaise. Let your creativity run wild with these little golden nuggets of protein.

Four ways of serving eggs: with corned beef, poached, eggs Benedict, and soft-boiled.

9
The Setting Hen

In no portion of the life cycle of chickens is the role of instinct so important as in the hatching of fertile eggs by a setting hen. We humans understand the mechanics of procreation so thoroughly that it is difficult for us to put ourselves in the position of the chicken, which plays out its role in the drama of life and death only in response to certain urgings, and without the vaguest idea of what it's doing or why.

Hens, we must suppose, have no suspicion that an egg is a potential chick. Even though chickens presumably don't have a wide repertoire of emotions (they hardly even get off on Beethoven's *Ninth,* for instance, or on the view from the front porch), laying seems to be a relatively emotional experience for hens—the ultimate high of bird-dom. When an egg is ready to be laid, a hen apparently begins to feel how nice it would be to find a secluded place to set in for a while. If she can find a place where there are already some eggs, so much the better. She doesn't realize that she is both assembling a clutch and hiding it from predators. Yet if either of these functions had been omitted, the chicken would have never been known to man, for it would never have endured those eons of survival of the fittest. Of course, the system is not perfect, and not all hens have equally strong instinctive urges. But nature makes up for inefficiency and waste by sheer numbers. Hundreds of times more eggs are laid than ever turn into adult chickens under natural circumstances; and it's a good thing too, or the world would long ago have drowned in chicken feathers.

Likewise, when a hen decides to set one warm spring day she has no idea that the warmth and humidity of her body provide just the right conditions for hatching the eggs below, that by leaving the nest briefly each day to eat she gives the eggs a much needed cooling period, and that when she returns and wiggles around in the nest to get comfortable, she inadvertently performs the essential task of turning the eggs. She sits night and day in a trance, snuggling the eggs to her. But by hatching time, she's just about tired of it all; and so, although the sudden transformation under her from eggs to chicks surely comes as somewhat of a surprise, it does seem to be a refreshing experience and she's simply tickled to death. She immediately develops an amiable relationship with the newcomers and enjoys cuddling them in her feathers or hustling them around in search of a choice tidbit.

If by chance the eggs are infertile or for some other reason fail to hatch, she will in time (perhaps another week or two) tire of the whole game, come out of her trance, abandon the nest, and resume her normal activities. It's not that she realizes it would be futile to remain on the eggs, but simply that, from her point of view, setting loses its charm after a time. Just as the de-

cision to set in the first place was not a rational one, the decision to stop setting is also instinctive. In this way, nature prevents hens from wasting energy on a lost cause.

PREPARING FOR SPRING

We prefer to hatch chicks early in the season—from the time egg laying gets into full swing until the beginning of summer. In northern areas it's best to delay hatching until the weather warms up a bit in late March or early April. Of course, eggs are available year-round, but the fertility of the parent stock is greatest in the spring, and in addition the overall quality of the chicks will be greater. We find that chicks hatched later in the season are generally smaller, not as vigorous, and don't grow as fast as early chicks. Besides, the later in the season they hatch, the greater are the chances that maturing birds will be put outside after the weather has gotten cold or rainy. Because they are still young and growing, they will run a greater risk of catching one of the diseases that lurk around in wet weather. Hens that get broody and attempt to set late in the season should be broken up and firmly discouraged from setting.

If several breeds of chickens run together most of the year and you want to raise chicks whose lineages you control, the first step to take as the hatching season approaches is to separate the chickens three weeks before eggs are to be collected for hatching. This is done to let sperm from random breedings in the barnyard clear from the hens' ovaries. If you don't mind raising mixed breeds, you won't have to worry about this. Of course, if bantams and large breeds run together you will end up with middle-sized chickens after a few years. Those who raise show stock have to be especially careful to keep track of the breeding (see Chapter 13, "Chickens for Show").

Although a flock should be free of mites and lice at all times, it is especially important to check for these vermin in the spring and to eliminate any before the chicks start to hatch (see the section on mites and lice in Chapter 14). In extreme cases, body parasites have been known to kill setting hens, and they certainly could kill baby chicks.

COLLECTING AND STORING EGGS

Some people stop collecting eggs and leave them all in the nests when they want their hens to set, hoping the hens will get broody. But we feel this is a waste of eggs. Left outside, the eggs may get broken or soiled, or the weather may be cold enough to freeze the eggs or warm enough for the embryos to begin partial but harmful development. The eggs may also rot. On the other hand, when eggs are collected and properly stored for hatching, they may still be eaten within a week. So if no hens go broody, the eggs won't have gone to waste.

Store eggs saved for hatching pointed end down in a cool, draft-free place. Nature permits a period of dormancy in eggs to allow a hen to collect a clutch together before she starts to set, so that all the chicks will hatch at the same time. A temperature of 40° to 60° F. will keep the embryos dormant. You should neither store them in the refrigerator nor try to keep them warm; the embryo will die at temperatures under 40° F. and may begin to decompose at temperatures over 60° F. We get best hatching results if we don't hold eggs for more than 7 days before setting them, although they can be kept up to 14 days with some success. After a week they will have to be turned once or twice a day, as the yolks tend to rise and might otherwise stick to the lining of the egg. Even if turned, hatchability starts to decrease after about a week. Some sources say the eggs should be turned daily from the first day, but we have had good hatches without doing this.

Be sure that the eggs you retain for hatching are from healthy, vigorous stock. Select eggs that are all the normal size and shape for their particular breed and that have thick shells with no cracks. Very large or oddly shaped eggs seldom hatch. Small eggs will produce small stock, so don't hatch them unless you deliberately want to decrease the size of your stock for some reason.

It is not possible to predetermine the sex of the chick that will hatch from any given egg, despite what some people think. A lady once gave us some eggs to hatch and told us, "I knew you'd want hens so I only brought you the ones that are going to hatch into hens." When we asked her, with veiled skepticism, how she knew, she gave us a demonstration: a set of keys held over an egg will soon start to swing—longitudinally if a rooster will hatch from the egg and transversally if a hen is to hatch from it. This is of course due to the magnetic forces coming out of the egg, she said. She got it straight from Mother Goose. If it were possible to sex eggs, commercial hatcheries could save a fortune by setting only eggs of the sex they need. This would save them incubator space, and they would never have a surplus of cockerels to dispose of.

It is helpful to mark each egg with the date (and breed, if you have more than one) when it is picked up. A wax pencil works well for marking the eggs: it's easy to read, won't rub off during the normal course of the hatch, and isn't likely to puncture the shell. It is best not to use fluid markers, as they might soak through the shell and possibly contaminate the egg or destroy the embryo. The reason for dating the eggs is to keep track of exactly how long they have been stored; in the event a hen doesn't get broody in time, you'll know which eggs are still good for hatching, which are only fair for hatching, and which are still safe to eat.

HENS FOR HATCHING

If you plan to use hens for hatching, you'll have to wait until one goes broody. We don't know of any way to *make* a hen broody, although darkened, undisturbed nests with a few dummy eggs in them may encourage broodiness to some extent. Some people close a hen up in a small cage with a bunch of eggs, but this will only upset her, and she may end up breaking the eggs in her attempt to get out.

You know you've got a broody hen when she stays on the nest, ruffles her feathers, and pecks your hand if you try to move her or take her eggs. She will set on fake eggs, or may even stay on an empty nest. We have one hen right now who thinks she's hatching three little green apples that she carefully rolled into her nest from under the tree. Setting hens seem almost hypnotized throughout the brooding period, maintaining a dreamy, vacant-eyed look. They get rather possessive about their eggs, carefully tucking under themselves any that roll away, and can be decidedly nasty in defending their eggs against any moving thing that comes near.

Each hen seems to follow a pattern in her setting habits. When you get to know your hens, you will be able to predict fairly accurately when each is likely to set, and how dependable each is as a setter and as a mother. Some hens never set. Chickens bred exclusively for egg production necessarily have had the brooding instinct bred out, although individual hens may occasionally want to set.

Some hens should not be allowed to set, even if they do get broody, either because they are not dependable during the hatching period or because they do not take proper care of their chicks once they hatch. If you want to prevent such hens from setting, or if you want to continue to collect eggs and therefore don't want your hens to set, you can try to break them up when they go broody. Depending on how determined a hen is, this is done by taking one of the following measures: taking the eggs away; repeatedly moving the hen off the nest; moving the nest; or, if all else fails, moving the hen to a different location. Since the incipient yolks within a hen are absorbed by her body while she is setting and egg laying then terminates, the sooner you break her up, the sooner she will be laying again.

If you want to be reasonably certain to have hens that will set, you might get a couple of hens of a type known to be especially dependable setters and good mothers. Many breeders of exotic birds use Silkies for hatching because they seem to have a strong instinct for setting and caring for their brood. Cochins also have strong brooding instincts as do common barnyard banties. If you can find someone who raises the breed you want, he should be able to tell you if they make good setters.

People sometimes inquire about buying a broody hen. A hen can be broody in one place and change her mind by the time she's moved. So if you're lucky enough to find someone who will sell you a broody hen, consider yourself doubly lucky if she continues to set once you've got her home. To help ensure that she will continue to set, move her at night and set her on dummy or unwanted eggs until you're sure she still wants to set.

We feel it's best to isolate setting hens from each other, as well as from the general flock. The hens might fight over the eggs; or, another hen may decide to lay an egg on the nest of a setting hen, confusing her when she comes back from eating and finds someone has taken her place. One year we had three hens all setting on the same nest, one on top of the other. One of the hens was somewhat larger, and it was really comical to see the other two peering out from under her wings like overgrown chicks. When the eggs hatched there were 22 baby chicks, which the 3 hens took collective care of. At night the little ones would go under whichever hen had the most room. We called them "the commune." This experience turned out well, but we haven't always been so lucky.

To avoid mix-ups, it's best to have separate hatching places where each setting hen will be alone. A nest for a hen to hatch her chicks in should be roomy enough to allow her to move around a little and turn her eggs; it should contain enough nesting litter for the hen to settle in and keep the eggs warm; and it should be placed where the chicks will be safe when they hatch and are ready to roam—for example, you don't want them to fall through the floor boards and not be able to get back up to their mother. The portable pen described at the end of Chapter 4, with a box of straw added, provides an excellent place for isolating a setting hen. When moving a broody hen, follow the same precautions mentioned for purchasing one: move her at night and give her a few eggs you don't care about until you are certain that she will continue to set in her new location. A hen that is not serious about her job of hatching chicks is wasting her time and your eggs.

Once you have determined that a hen is serious about setting, put the eggs you want hatched under her, but don't give her so many that any are sticking out around the edges. If one sticks out and gets chilled, she'll rotate it back in and leave another out to chill so that the whole batch will be lost. We find that about 8 to 10 eggs under a banty or 12 to 15 under a larger hen is plenty, but it depends somewhat on the types of eggs you're setting and on the size of the hen. You have to remember, too, that once the chicks hatch they all have to fit under the mother hen at night. Keep a record of when you set the eggs, and expect your new chicks in 21 days.

Setting hens leave the nest occasionally to eat, drink, and eliminate. Luckily, the eggs need a few minutes to cool down each day, so don't be alarmed if you see your setting hen off the nest. When she gets back on, she'll wiggle around to get comfortable and thereby inadvertently perform the necessary operation of turning the eggs. (In an incubator, the cooling and turning must be done artificially.) She should return within 30 minutes, though a bit longer won't endanger the eggs; after the first few days, however, a long period of cooling will kill the developing embryos. If your setting hen is not getting off the nest at all, be sure she has plenty of food and water within reach. Feeding her grains only (no mash) will keep her droppings solid and prevent the eggs from getting very soiled.

HENS AS FOSTER MOTHERS

If you don't have a rooster but want to raise chicks, you could purchase some fertile eggs and set them under your broody hen. She won't know the difference and will hatch them as if they were her own. But be sure to give them to her fairly soon after she has begun to set; a hen that is kept on the nest much more than 21 days may lose interest and decide to quit. Tips and cautions on purchasing eggs for hatching are included in Chapter 15, "Starting Your Flock."

You could even set eggs of other fowl under a hen. She doesn't care and will mother anything that hatches under her. (But she *will* be alarmed if her babies jump into the water and start swimming around!) Some eggs, such as duck and goose eggs, do take longer to hatch and, although we've seen many

cases where hens have hatched them successfully, there's always the chance that the hen won't sit it out that long. And don't try to set a huge goose egg under a bitty little banty hen or a clutch of tiny fragile quail eggs under a large New Hampshire Red. We've also found that in some cases you'd best be prepared to gather up the newly hatched young as soon as they fluff out and raise them yourself. For whatever reason, young birds of certain species—guineas, peafowl, and wild ducks, for example—don't always respond to the hen's motherly clucking and will wander off to die of exposure.

Even if you don't have a rooster and you know your hen's eggs are infertile, the hen doesn't share that knowledge and may very well go broody and insist on setting a clutch anyway. Or she may set on eggs which, for reasons neither she nor you know, turn out to be unhatchable. Or she may set on an empty nest. In any case the natural culmination of the brooding period will not occur, and you may eventually find yourself wishing to give your hen a brood of chicks to mother which she didn't hatch herself. You might have to purchase chicks for this purpose if they are not otherwise available to you. Information on purchasing chicks can be found in Chapter 15.

Wait until a hen has been setting for three weeks before giving her the chicks. (Add a day or two if you think her eggs may have been fertile, in case they're late hatchers.) Don't try to give chicks to her much sooner than they would naturally have hatched under her, as she may not be psychologically ready for them. Above all, never present a hen with a batch of chicks without the preparatory brooding period, as she would probably kill them. A hen must be put in the mood for motherhood by being allowed to set. This psychological change is as important a result of a hen's setting as the actual incubation of the eggs, for without it hatched chicks would be left motherless.

Not only must the hen accept the chicks, but it is also just as essential that the chicks be snookered into accepting the hen as Mom. Timing is just as critical in getting this to happen. The chicks should be day-old. If they are older it may be too late for them to recognize and identify with the hen you have selected for their foster mother.

To increase the chances that a hen will accept the chicks as her own, slip them under her at night. While you're at it, remove whatever she was setting on. (It is *not* necessary to leave eggshells strewn about the nest to complete the charade.)

There is always the hazard that the hen will not accept the chicks, so watch carefully the first day in case they need to be rescued, and be prepared to raise them yourself should she reject them.

THE NEW BROOD

However she acquires them, the mother hen will take care of the chicks once she accepts them, and there's not much you have to do other than make sure that there is plenty of fresh water within their reach and that they have something available to eat. Mother hens running loose seem to find plenty of food for their chicks, although you may wish to give them finely ground scratch or high-protein feed as a supplement. When they are confined you should definitely give them a high-protein starting feed. The mother hen will eat it, too, so make sure there's enough. Or you might get a special chick feeder, which has openings big enough for chicks to eat through but too small for grown chickens. A chick feeding program is outlined in Chapter 11, "The Care and Feeding of Chicks."

Besides avoiding disasters during the incubation period, a further reason for isolating the setting hen is to protect the chicks once they hatch. When preparing a place to confine the chicks, remember that they're about 90 percent fluff and can squeeze through the most incredibly small holes. The chicks can be turned out with their mother to join the rest of the flock after a month or so, when they've gotten all their feathers. Confining very small chicks will prevent marauders from getting at them, as well as protect them from being pecked by some of the other chickens. We don't know why, but sometimes the big guys can be pretty mean to the little ones. Mother hens will even peck a chick from another brood if it gets too close. Once we decided to save space by putting two mother hens with their broods together in one cage. We noticed that the chicks of one of the hens were getting weak and listless while the other brood was thriving. After watching for a while we discovered that one mother had claimed the territory that included the food and water containers and wouldn't let the other hen's chicks near them. (Needless to say, we managed to find another cage where the chicks could regain their strength.)

If a person is totally unacquainted with the nature of birds, the first hatch can be a traumatic experience. We heard of a lady who bought a mother hen with chicks from friends. She called a few days later to complain that the chicks were dying. It turned out she hadn't given them anything to eat, but she blamed the hen: the lady said she discovered the problem when she checked and found that the hen's milk had all dried up! It was discreetly pointed out to her that chickens are not mammals and do not have mammary glands.

10
Incubating

It is always easier to leave the hassle of incubation to the hens, and those that stick it out have uncanny success. But some are just not reliable setters, and when you've lost a few clutches to an incompetent hen, you may in your frustration turn to artificial incubation.

There are always more eggs laid than your hens could possibly hatch, even if you let them, and the surplus can be eaten, sold, or hatched in an incubator. Or you may wish to begin your flock by purchasing eggs and hatching them yourself. In any case, artificial incubation may suit your hatching needs.

If you have eggs that you want hatched, but don't have the time or the inclination to bother with an incubator, you might be able to find someone who custom hatches eggs. They usually advertise in the poultry section of the classified ads or on feed store bulletin boards. A small fee may be charged for each egg set or each egg that hatches, or the hatcher may want to split the hatch with you. Be sure to settle in advance what your obligation will be.

THE INCUBATOR

You may want to make your own incubator. If you're handy at building things and understand the principles involved in the incubating process, you should be able to build a satisfactory incubator. However, simulating the conditions under a broody hen takes a bit of ingenuity, so if tinkering just isn't your thing, you might rather purchase one ready-made. Plans for building a rudimentary incubator are included in the circulars "From Egg to Chick" and "The Avian Embryo," listed in the Appendix. Incubator kits can be purchased from some feed stores as well as through mail-order poultry suppliers.

Sometimes secondhand incubators are advertised at feed stores or in the classified ads. A little work may be needed to get them running properly, but if the structure is sound and the price is right, it's usually worth it.

Factory-assembled incubators are available with capacities ranging from half-a-dozen eggs to thousands. Some incubators have glass tops or sides through which you can watch the entire hatch. These models are especially good for classroom use. Farm catalogs also advertise incubators. Or, you could go straight to any of the several incubator manufacturing companies. Some are listed in the Appendix.

Because incubators come in such a variety of types, instructions for their use will vary somewhat. Follow the manufacturer's suggestions for whatever type you have. Your local agricultural or cooperative extension service office may also have information that will help you get started.

If you come by a secondhand incubator for which the instructions have been lost, try to find out who made it and what the model number is, and write the manufacturer asking for another instruction manual. They will usually be glad to send one. If you can't find out exactly which kind you have, look through the catalogs and find the one that most nearly looks like yours.

In case you're curious about what is involved, we'll explain how incubators operate. However, each particular model may have special additional requirements; this explanation is not intended as a substitute for the manufacturer's manual, but as a supplement.

The most common incubators for home use are either the forced-air (fan-ventilated) type, or the still-air (gravity-ventilated) type. Forced-air incubators usually provide better control over hatching conditions. A fan keeps the air circulating so that the temperature will remain constant throughout, and closable vents are provided to help regulate the humidity. This type comes in small models but can also be purchased in larger

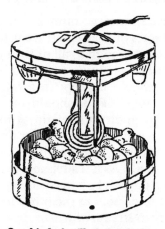

One kind of still-air incubator.

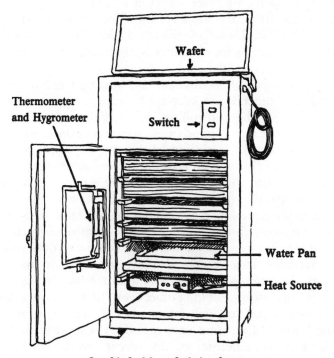

One kind of forced-air incubator.

cabinet models made for large numbers of eggs. Still-air incubators come in all sorts of shapes but are usually small, with the heating element close enough to all of the eggs to keep them a uniform temperature. The incubator should be kept in a room with a constant temperature of about 70°F. It should not be located near a window, a heater, or in direct sunlight. A forced-air incubator will usually operate properly even when the conditions in the room are less than perfect, whereas more caution must be used with a still-air incubator. As it is advisable to check the temperature several times a day, it's best to locate the incubator where it will be convenient to do so. On the other hand, keep the incubator out of the main stream of traffic, where nobody can trip on the cord and accidently unplug it and where visitors will not be likely to open it up to see what's inside. Many people who see ours for the first time think it's an old-time refrigerator, and we're always afraid someone will open it looking for a cold beer. If we're expecting a lot of company, we tape a note to the door asking that it not be opened.

In both types of incubators, the heating element is thermostatically controlled to keep the interior temperature within certain limits. The controlling device, called a wafer, is an ether-filled disc that expands and contracts as the temperature goes up and down. It is essential that a spare wafer be handy because, either through an accident or through long usage, the wafer sometimes springs a leak and the ether goes out of it. Wafers invariably go out in the middle of the night or on Sunday when the stores are closed. They are available at some feed stores and through most farm catalogs. Sometimes incubators take an uncommon type of wafer, so compare yours with the ones available locally, and if they don't match up, check through the catalogs until you find a source for the right kind. A wafer may last quite a long time, even through several hatching seasons. But you will know when it has gone out—the temperature will increase very rapidly. If the wafer has been out for some time before you discover it, chances are the eggs have been cooked. If you should happen to catch it right away, however, allow the eggs to cool down by leaving the incubator open for a while. Change the wafer, start the incubator back up, and hope that you were in time to save the hatch.

Although somewhat less likely, another cause of sudden change in temperature is a faulty or dirty thermal switch. This switch is what the wafer presses against as it expands and releases as it contracts, causing the heat to go off and on. It's handy to have a spare switch around.

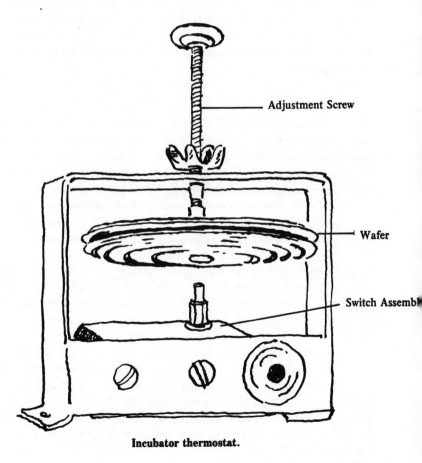

Incubator thermostat.

Incidentally, remember that your electrical power supply might fail at any time due to a storm or malfunction, and the local power company is not legally liable for providing you with continuous power service. Have an emergency plan to protect your eggs if a power failure should occur. If it's really important to you not to lose your hatch, have a standby generator ready or know where you can obtain one. Other options are covering the incubator with a down sleeping bag, heavy quilts, or blankets; building a fire near the incubator if feasible; moving the incubator near the fireplace; or if your home heating is not electric, turning it way up. Whatever you choose to do, close monitoring of the internal temperature of the incubator is essential during such a crisis, since no thermostatic device is functioning.

THE EGGS

At the beginning of Chapter 9, "The Setting Hen," we made some comments about collecting and storing eggs for hatching: hatch only in the spring, separate your different breeds, select the best eggs for high hatchability, mark eggs with date and breed, store them in a cool place but not too long, and so forth. These remarks apply to collecting and storing eggs for incubator hatching just as well as for hatching under hens. We recommend that you do not simply stick every egg into the incubator as it is laid. You will soon see that saving the eggs over a period of time and putting them in all at once makes it much easier to keep track of your hatch and also makes it likelier the hatch will be successful. If you are planning to purchase eggs for hatching instead of using your own, consult Chapter 15, "Starting Your Flock," for suggestions.

Very dirty eggs carry harmful bacteria and should not be put into the incubator. Clean them without washing them, if possible; wipe off any droppings that may be on an egg before they harden and stick. If an egg has to be cleaned, try to scrape the dirt off with steel wool, sandpaper, or a small wire kitchen brush. If that doesn't do it, wipe it with a damp cloth. If it *must* be washed, use warm water and dry immediately. Washing will remove the natural bloom and may even force bacteria into the egg. Some hatchers prefer to incubate dirty eggs rather than run a risk by washing them. Others don't want dirties in the incubator, but feel that washed eggs won't hatch, and so simply dispose of them. Our policy is to wash eggs carefully when they really need it, and leave the rest to the Easter Bunny.

The eggs should not be crowded into the incubator. Don't try to set more eggs than the manufacturer intended. The racks on the trays of a cabinet incubator keep the eggs properly spaced. The eggs should be positioned with the small pointed end slightly downward. Failure to keep the small end down may cause the chicks to be deformed. If the chicks pip, or break through, the small end of the shell, then you probably weren't careful about keeping the smaller end lower than the larger. Pipping should always occur at the large end, where the air cell is. Otherwise, the chick will probably die.

TEMPERATURE

The temperature at which the incubator should be operated will depend on what kind you have and on what kind of eggs you want to hatch. Departures from the proper hatching temperature can cause disfigured chicks. For example, chicks sometimes have crooked toes or nonfunctioning legs when they hatch. For chicken eggs, most forced-air incubators should run at 99.5° F. and most still-air incubators at 102° F.; however, the proper thermometer reading often depends on where in the incubator the thermometer is located. If a ther-

Incubator thermometer.

mometer is not exactly where it was originally intended to be, variations are likely. For instance, after several hatches we found that our old forced-air incubator works best when the thermometer reads 100° F. Because the incubator thermometer is near the peep window, it may not be giving the actual temperature of the eggs, especially if the room is unusually hot or cold. Although the thermometer reading may vary with the circumstances, the actual egg temperature required for optimum hatch is always the same.

Adjust the temperature a day or two before setting the eggs. Turning the wafer adjustment screw to move it toward the switch lowers the temperature and vice versa. Once the required temperature is attained, leave the thermostat control alone unless there is drastic fluctuation and it needs readjusting. Constantly playing with the thermostat can wreak havoc with the hatch. Expect the temperature to drop when you put in a batch of eggs and to return gradually to operating level as the eggs warm up. Always leave all the trays in a cabinet model, even empty ones, so that the air flow will be maintained as the manufacturer intended.

Use only a special hatching thermometer in the incubator. Indoor-outdoor thermometers are not suited to this purpose. The spacing between degrees is wider in the special thermometer, making it easier to read fractions of a degree. You should be able to detect a temperature change of a quarter of a degree F. A new incubator will have a thermometer in it, but if yours gets lost or broken, another can be purchased anywhere incubators are sold and at some feed stores.

HUMIDITY

A forced-air incubator generally has a wet-bulb hygrometer which measures the humidity in wet-bulb degrees, whereas the hygrometer in a still-air incubator measures the percentage of relative humidity. For chicken eggs, a forced-air incubator should be kept at around 86° F. wet-bulb and a still-air incubator at about 60 percent relative humidity. Small incubators often do not have a hygrometer because of the impracticality of taking up extra space, so the size of the air cells in the eggs is used as a moisture indicator. Even if a device to monitor humidity is present, it is wise to use the air-cell size as an independent check. We explain this further in the section on candling, below.

Humidity must be provided to prevent excess loss of natural moisture within the eggs. Incubators usually have a pan in the bottom that should be kept full of water. Sometimes the pan is divided into sections. By filling more of the sections you will increase the surface area of the water, thus increasing the amount of evaporation and, vice versa. Keep the water level up by adding warm water as needed, when you do the turning. On the last three days before the hatch, increase the humidity by adding another water pan, by lightly sprinkling the eggs with warm water, by putting some clean wet sponges on the tray near the eggs, or by closing some of the vents of a forced-air incubator. The hygrometer reading should be about 91° F. wet-bulb or 70 percent relative humidity during the actual hatch.

TURNING

Unless your incubator has an automatic turning device, you will have to turn the eggs by hand. This is done to keep the developing embryo from sticking to the lining, which would arrest its development. Mother hens turn their eggs instinctively about every 15 minutes. Eggs in an incubator with an automatic turning device can be turned once every hour. Since turning by hand is more than a little nuisance, it needn't be done that frequently, but three times a day is the absolute minimum. You should turn the eggs at evenly spaced intervals. To help us remember, we turn ours right after breakfast, on getting home from work, and just before going to bed. If you can work it into your schedule, more than three daily turnings would be better. Eggs should be turned an odd number of times each day, though, in order that on consecutive days the position of the eggs during the long overnight periods can be alternated. Be sure not to miss a lot of turnings in a row, and avoid turning at irregular intervals.

In incubators without racks, turning can be done by rolling the eggs around with the palm of the hand. To be sure you've turned all of the eggs all the way over, mark an "X" on one side of each egg and an "O" on the opposite side. After turning, all of the eggs should have the same side up. Try not to jar them unduly while turning—a shock may rupture the blood vessels within the embryo. Wash your hands well before turning so that body oils and dirt won't get on the eggs and seal up the pores.

Incubators with racks usually have turning wires to facilitate turning. There is one wire for every two trays. The wire is pulled out of one tray and pushed into the next. These only work when hatching exactly the size eggs that the racks were designed to hold. Eggs of any other size must be turned individually by hand.

A forced-air incubator should always be turned off, with the fan stopped completely, before the door is opened. By all means, don't forget to turn it back on when you're done! A still-air incubator should be left running when opened.

The eggs are turned from the 2nd to the 18th day. Then, turning is stopped to give the chicks a chance to orient themselves and figure out where they are going to pip.

COOLING

Most instructions say to cool the eggs for 15 minutes each day. We find that opening the incubator to turn the eggs cools them sufficiently, but then we have a large incubator and it takes a while to turn all the eggs. In any case, if the temperature has gone up a bit for any reason, it's a good idea to open the incubator for a short time to allow the eggs to cool down.

CANDLING

The eggs should be candled after one week of incubation to see that they are developing properly. Those that aren't should be discarded. Speckled eggs are more difficult to candle than plain-shelled eggs, especially when the embryo is still very small, so it is sometimes necessary to wait a little longer before inspecting them. If the eggs have been accidentally chilled or overheated, you can candle them to see whether they are still okay. By waiting a few days before candling, you can determine more definitely if the embryo has died and also minimize the harmful effects of subjecting eggs that are already jeopardized to another change in temperature.

We use a slide projector for a candling box, holding the egg up to the lens to reveal its entire contents. A simple candling box can be made by cutting a hole smaller than the eggs in a cardboard box and suspending a light bulb inside. The only light coming out of the box should be through the hole. Candling is most easily done in a darkened room. Work rapidly while candling to avoid chilling the eggs. When candling from a cabinet incubator, remove one tray at a time and restart the incubator while candling each tray.

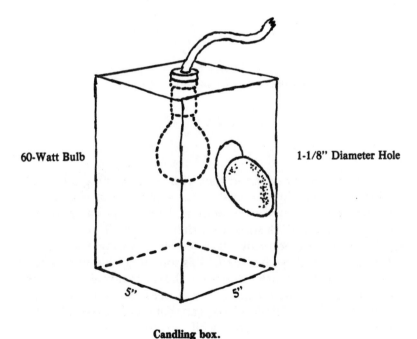

60-Watt Bulb   1-1/8" Diameter Hole

5"   5"

Candling box.

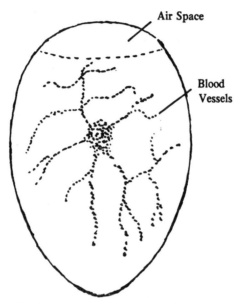

Fertile egg, one week after incubation.

If you see a tiny dark red spot with veins running out in all directions, you're in business! If the egg is clear, it is either infertile or the embryo was weak and died very early. If the yolk appears as a dark shadow or there are grayish clouds, the egg is rotting. A blood-ring (dark red circle with no veins) indicates that the embryo has died. This sometimes happens when the storing temperature was wrong, the incubator temperature was irregular, or the fertilization was weak. Spoiling eggs give off harmful gases and use up oxygen that is better saved for the hatching eggs. Once in a great while a rotting egg will explode, sending out a spray of gooey stinky stuff that's not only a real mess to clean up but may contaminate the other eggs as well. So, it is important to candle and remove any eggs that aren't developing properly.

Candling can also tell you if the humidity is right. Compare the air cell in the big end of the egg to the diagram on this page. If the air cell is larger, provide more moisture; if smaller, decrease the amount of moisture.

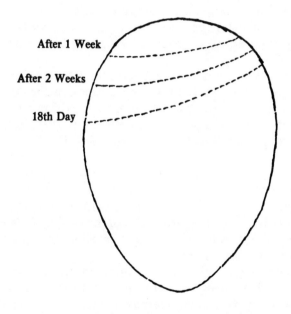

After 1 Week

After 2 Weeks

18th Day

Changing air space in a developing egg.

THE HATCH

Keep the hatching eggs on the lower trays of a cabinet incubator so that, as the hatch progresses, the down that newly hatched chicks shed won't get all over the other trays. Also, the wastes from inside the shells won't get on the eggs beneath them, and the general mess will be easier to clean out after each hatch. Some incubators have a special hatching section, making cleanup a little easier.

Chicks will usually hatch on the 21st day after the eggs were set, although it may be a day earlier if you have particularly vigorous stock. If your incubator temperature has been a little high, they will hatch sooner; if low, they will hatch later. Eggs that were all set at the same time should hatch around the same time—within about 24 hours after pipping begins. If some of the eggs had an early start because a hen had been setting on them before you collected the eggs, they'll hatch sooner than the others.

If a lot of chicks pip without actually hatching, the humidity is probably not high enough. In most cases nothing can be done for the present hatch: since chick tissue hardens within a very short time after the chick pips, a chick helped out of the shell long after it has pipped is likely to be deformed. But for succeeding hatches, follow the suggestions in the section on humidity (earlier in this chapter) for raising the humidity during the hatch. If you notice that only one or two chicks have pipped but haven't hatched, it's still best not to attempt to help them out. Weak chicks have trouble getting out of the shell and often die even if helped out. But if they do live, by allowing them to hatch you will weaken your stock.

Avoid the temptation of repeatedly opening the incubator to watch the hatch in progress. This will chill the eggs and drastically lower the humidity, thereby ruining what might have been a good hatch. Most incubators have windows through which you can see at least a little—if you peer hard enough and use a flashlight. If you are the type of person who must see every detail, get an incubator with glass sides or top.

After the chicks are hatched, leave them in the incubator for 12 to 24 hours, until they fluff out. The chicks will be wet when they hatch, and exposure to cold air would chill them. When they have thoroughly dried, remove them to a brooder. Be sure to check the floor of a cabinet incubator for chicks that may have fallen out of the trays. During the first 24 to 48 hours the chicks are still assimilating the yolk, or food sac of the egg, and do not need to be fed. In fact, our experience has been that giving them food or water prematurely might harm them. Sheets of newspaper should be used as litter on the brooder floor for the first few days, until the chicks learn to eat what you feed them instead of the litter. How to raise your new chicks is detailed in Chapter 11, "The Care and Feeding of Chicks."

Remove the loose chick down from the incubator after each hatch. Down in the water pan reduces the evaporating surface and will lower the humidity. A damp sponge will pick up quite a bit of the down in the bottom of the incubator, and a vacuum cleaner can be used if the down is loose and dry. Remove the empty eggshells and any unhatched eggs. The shells can be crushed and fed to the chickens.

It is rare for every egg that is set to hatch, and there are so many factors involved that it is often impossible to determine exactly why. Among other things, the vitality of the parent stock could have been low, due to poor diet, old age, disease, or heredity; the hen-to-rooster ratio could have been too high; the eggs could have been stored incorrectly or for too long; or the incubator could have been operated improperly. Exact details for operating an incubator vary with the individual circumstances (such as temperature of the room and amount of insulation in the incubator), so a small amount of experimenting is sometimes necessary before good results are obtained.

At the end of each hatching season, clean the incubator thoroughly with a good disinfectant, and then air it out well before storing so that bacteria will not have a chance to develop and flourish in it over the winter.

CONTINUOUS HATCHING

The very best way to hatch is to let each setting of eggs finish hatching before starting another. Don't open the incubator for the first day while the eggs are warming up. Turn them from the 2nd to the 18th day, and then raise the humidity and keep the incubator closed until the chicks have hatched. The incubator can then be easily cleaned out and a fresh hatch started. The success rate will be much greater with this method. However, it is often impractical to hatch this way because settings could only be made once every three weeks, unless more than one incubator is used.

So if you want to hatch more eggs at once, you can practice continuous hatching—having overlapping hatches in the same incubator, with some eggs hatching while others are still developing. Because hatching is less successful with this method, it is rarely recommended by incubator manufacturers, but many people do it with good results. We like to set our eggs once a week. Seven days is the longest eggs should be stored for good hatchability anyway, and setting on the same day every week helps us keep track of our hatches. We identify each hatch with a special mark so that we can tell at a glance which eggs are on which team. We draw a longitudinal ring around each egg in one week's hatch, a transverse ring around another's, and no ring around the third's. In a cabinet incubator, the different hatches can be put on separate trays, with a piece of masking tape bearing the date of hatch on each tray.

We also find it very helpful to keep a hatching calendar to record when each setting was made, when to stop turning them, and when they will hatch. When we turn the eggs each morning, we check the calendar to see what's supposed to happen that day.

During the last three days before a hatch, special care should be taken to avoid moisture loss and chilling when the incubator is opened to turn eggs in succeeding hatches. This means working rapidly. If you're using a still-air incubator, the eggs are more exposed, so use a clean, warm, damp hand towel to cover the about-to-hatch eggs while the incubator is open. When hatching continuously in either type of incubator, treat eggs as described earlier: stop turning on the 18th day, thereafter sprinkling them lightly with warm water and placing damp sponges nearby. Some manufacturers recommend adding an extra water pan to increase the humidity on the last two days before each hatch, then dropping the humidity below normal for the two days after the hatch to permit succeeding hatches to dry down to the proper level. We have tried this and find that it does improve the hatch somewhat. In this case, special care must be taken to ensure that succeeding hatches are neither kept too moist for too long (preventing moisture from escaping on schedule) nor dried out excessively (causing moisture to escape too rapidly).

SUMMARY

Even though we've hatched a goodly number of eggs, we still get excited each time we hear peeps in the incubator. Because proper procedure is essential for a successful hatch, and because we want you to experience the same thrill we get with each week's hatch, we have provided the following outline to help you remember the steps. Happy hatching!

1) Select eggs carefully
2) Store the eggs—small end down
                    at 40° to 60° F.
                    for no more than two weeks (and
                          preferably no more than one)
                    turning daily after the first week
3) Temperature:
        99.5° F. in forced-air incubator
        102° F. in still-air incubator
4) Humidity:
        86° F. wet-bulb in forced-air incubator
        60 percent relative humidity in still-air incubator
5) Turn eggs three times daily from 2nd to 18th day
6) Candle eggs after first week
7) Raise humidity on last three days:
        91° F. wet-bulb in forced-air incubator
        70 percent relative humidity in still-air incubator
8) Leave chicks in incubator until fluffed out
9) Clean up after each hatch

Stages of development inside the shell.

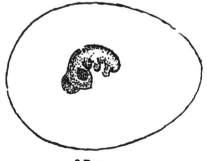

9 Days   12 Days

19 Days

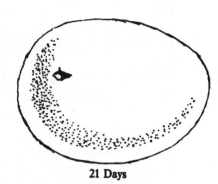

21 Days

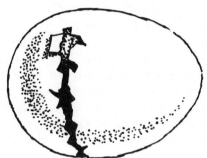

Pipping

11
The Care and Feeding of Chicks

If you plan to have hens do all of your hatching, they will take care of the details of raising the chicks (though we hope you have read Chapter 9, "The Setting Hen," so you won't have any nasty surprises). But if you will be hatching in an incubator, or purchasing chicks, then all of the joys of motherhood will be conferred on you. Men will have to consent to be mothers too, as baby chicks have no use for fathers.

If we hadn't spent hours out in the yard watching baby chicks, we would never have realized how well equipped for life baby birds are by comparison with babies of other animals. Sure, the chicks need to be warmed up from time to time, especially at night and when the weather is inclement. And they need protection and a little help from their mothers in finding food. But it is remarkable that baby chicks can walk and scamper about immediately upon hatching and can fly within a week. They can see and they know how to eat; they can even understand a complete chicken vocabulary that includes cries of distress, the clucked expressions of motherly contentment, and calls meaning "hawk—run" and "food—come." They fight too, just like daddy roosters! In comparison, baby cats, rabbits, and people may be blind, helpless, mute, or immobile for weeks or even years.

Chicks that you raise will need some sort of brooder in which they can be kept warm and safe while they are growing. If you plan on raising chicks only once or raising only a few each year, you can use a cardboard box for a brooder. If you plan to raise a lot of chicks each year you might find that a permanent brooder is a good investment, as trying to keep an adequate supply of the right-size cardboard boxes on hand is a nuisance. A permanent brooder can be homemade once you know the principles involved. The less wood and the more wire and metal parts you use in the construction, the easier it will be to keep clean. The brooder will have to be cleaned often during the hatching season and should be disinfected each year before it is stored away.

Brooders can be purchased from most places that sell incubators and come in a variety of sizes and types. The kind you should get will partly depend on how many and what kind of chicks you raise, but often your choice will be further narrowed by what is being sold locally or what is available secondhand.

For a simple homemade brooder, all you need is a cardboard box with a layer of litter or newspaper in the bottom, which should be changed frequently. Partially cover the top with newspaper or cardboard to help keep out drafts and still allow some fresh air in. A light bulb suspended in the box provides heat. The bulb should be far enough away from the edges of the box that it won't start a fire. We screw the bulb into a spotlight reflector with a clamp to hold it in place; such reflectors with clamps are available in hardware stores.

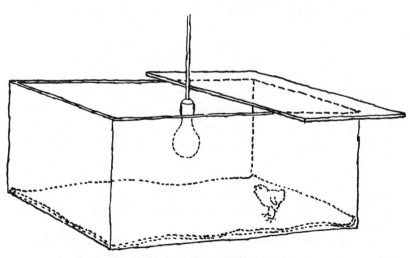

Homemade brooder.

The size of the box will depend on the size and number of chicks you intend to put in it and will have to be increased as the chicks grow. The chicks should have plenty of room to move around and to spread out to sleep. They should also have enough room to get away from the heat of the bulb if they need to. If they pant or press against the corners and edges of the box, away from the bulb, they are too hot and could possibly suffocate. Reduce the wattage of the bulb or get a bigger box. If the chicks huddle together in a pile under the bulb, they are chilly. The bulb could be too high to provide enough heat, the wattage could be too low, or the box could be too large and drafty. If chicks huddle overnight or for any long period, they may be smothered in large quantities.

The temperature in the brooder should start around 90° F. for newly hatched chicks and be decreased by about 5° F. each week. But you don't really need a thermometer. You'll be able to tell the chicks are happy by their contented peeps. If they are in distress from cold or hunger, their loud insistent cheeping will tip you off. Within comfortable limits, the more rapidly the brooder temperature is reduced, the more quickly the chicks will feather out. Comfortable chicks will pursue their normal activities of walking around, pecking at the food, pecking at the sides of the box, drinking water, and sleeping. They need quite a lot of rest and will frequently lie about like a carpet on the brooder floor, with their heads down and wings spread out. A friend once spent the night in the living room, where we kept a small brooder. The chicks were very active and lively when he went to sleep, but in the morning they were all spread out motionless on the floor of the brooder. The alarmed friend came rushing into our room to announce that all the chicks had died in the night. Meanwhile, his commotion had awakened the chicks. When we went to the living room to examine the death scene, our friend was confounded to see that the chicks had come back to life and were just as active as they had been the night before.

Chicks are prone to catching a number of chickhood diseases, so proper sanitation in the brooder is essential to keeping them healthy. Provide a new box with fresh litter every couple of days. The litter should never be allowed to remain damp; if water is spilled the litter should be cleaned out. Chicks are especially susceptible to coccidiosis, and if it gets started in your brood you could lose almost all the chicks. Some chicks that survive may still carry the disease dormant in their systems; when the pullets reach laying age, the additional stress may be too much for their bodies and they will succumb unexpectedly.

Chicks must have clean, fresh water available to them at all times. You can buy plastic or metal watering basins that fit onto mason jars and are ideal for watering chicks. The screw-on type is less likely to get tipped over as the chicks grow and get more

Chick waterer.

and more frisky. Tippy water containers can be stabilized by placing a stone or clean gravel in them. If you wish to use some other type of water container, be sure the chicks cannot walk in it or fall into it. Chicks sometimes drown from being mashed into the water dish by their brooder-mates, and they may get some of their droppings into the water if they can walk in it. They may also get water in the litter and feed, causing unpleasant odors as well as promoting the spread of disease. If they do manage to get water in their feed, replace it before it gets moldy. Feeding them only a little at a time, but often, helps in keeping the feed clean.

Chicks should be started on a special high-protein ration. It is usually available both with and without a medication that inhibits coccidiosis. If you don't use medicated feed for baby chicks, you run the risk that coccidiosis will attack your chicks and possibly wipe out as many as 90 percent of them. It may be discontinued with relative safety after about eight weeks, as by then the chicks are building up a natural immunity. Continued use of the medicated feed after 12 weeks is definitely not advisable, since it may interfere with the development of this natural immunity. The chicks should, however, be kept on the nonmedicated high-protein feed from then until they have attained full size if they are to grow rapidly and stay healthy. As they reach maturity you may gradually switch them over to your adult feeding program (see Chapter 6, "Feeding Your Flock"). If for any reason you don't wish to use the medicated feed, sanitation should be of increased concern—the brooder will have to be well cleaned at least twice a week so that the disease-causing organisms will not be allowed to mature and become infectious.

If at some point you wish to start feeding scratch to your young birds, a special little-guy's version is available that is chopped up very small. Some people like to feed greens to small chicks, but this sometimes causes loose droppings and we don't recommend it. You could feed them a few worms or bugs from the garden. They'll love it; in fact, they'll act like they're about to die of ecstasy.

Chick feeder.

Chick feeders can be purchased at the feed store or through farm catalogs. But for a small number of chicks, an empty tuna can or large jar lid may be used.

Chicks sometimes develop a condition called pasting up, which happens when their droppings are loose and stick to the vent area. After a while there is a buildup of hardened material, and the chick is no longer able to eliminate. If you see this happening, pick the dried droppings off. Some of the chick's down may be pulled off too, and the chick won't like that at all. But if you work very gently, discomfort will be kept to a minimum, and the chick will be happier in the long run. If pasting up affects a large percentage of chicks, a disease could be the cause. Make sure you are providing sanitary conditions and proper feed. If pasting persists or the chicks begin to die, you might want to consult a vet or an experienced poultry raiser in your area.

You should plan to house the chicks inside for four to six weeks. However, chicks produce a fine dust that will settle on everything, so if you have them in the house you might want to keep the brooder in a small room or closet with the door shut to prevent the dust from spreading. While raising our first brood of chicks, we had all sorts of family disputations over when the house was going to get cleaned, even when it had been only a half hour since the last dusting. After the chicks were put outside, the problem disappeared and the cause became apparent. Chicks can be kept in a garage or other outbuilding with electricity, provided it is draft-free as well as cat- and child-proof. If you have children, explain to them that chicks need a lot of rest and that they can be loved to death by squeezing little hands.

When the chicks are a week or two old, they can be put outside for a while on warm days. If you have a few chicks, you might put them on the lawn and stay with them. This helps teach the chicks to recognize you so that they'll more quickly become your pets. Chickens, like other pets, can become fond of their owners. They come when you call them, follow you around, and sit by you when you're pursuing outdoor activities such as reading in the sunshine or working in the garden. We even know several people who keep them as house pets. They claim that chickens are especially fond of watching television!

If there are too many chicks to keep an eye on, or if you don't have the time to watch over them, put them in a pen such as the one described at the end of Chapter 4, "The Coop." This will protect them from cats and other marauders and keep them from wandering away. They can then safely scratch in the dirt or peck at weeds and bugs, and they'll love it. The cage should be moved each day so that they have a fresh place in which to scratch. Be sure there is some shade so that the chicks can get out of the hot sun if they want to.

As they grow older, the chicks may be left outside for longer and longer periods, but still should be brought in each night so they won't chill. When the weather has warmed sufficiently and the chicks have most of their feathers (at about four to six weeks), you can put them out permanently; if it is convenient to hang a light bulb for warmth, you can put the chicks out a little sooner. We like to check on our chicks several times during their first few nights out to be sure they aren't huddling and smothering each other. Chicks should not be put together with older chickens right away as they might get picked on. The plans at the end of Chapter 4 provide some ideas for housing young birds.

Chicks begin to think about perching at night when they are four to six weeks old, and it's a good idea to get them into the habit early by providing small, low perches. It sure is cute to see all those miniature chickens roosting just like the grown-ups.

Occasionally information is published on how to sex chicks, but with the small number of chicks raised each year on which to practice, the average person seldom attains any great degree of accuracy. However, even amateurs can usually distinguish the sex of their chicks after a week or two. The accuracy may still be far from 100 percent, but it's fun to try to figure out what you have. Some of the cockerels will have little combs sticking up and little pink wattles, while pullets generally show little development until they're older. However, some kinds of cockerels will not show development until later, and pullets of a breed known especially for laying may develop combs and wattles much sooner than other breeds. In any case, by the time the chicks are three to eight weeks of age, depending on the breed, you should be able to tell the sex for sure. The cockerels are usually larger than the pullets, their combs and wattles will be

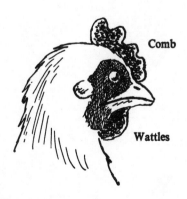

Comb

Wattles

Comb and wattles developing on a six-week cockerel.

redder, and their development is decidedly more pronounced.

All through their chickhood, and even into maturity, chickens are prone to develop the disgusting habit of eating each other. Be sure to read the section on cannibalism in Chapter 14 so that you can take measures to prevent its occurrence among your chicks, and be prepared to deal with it if it should happen.

If you hatch a new brood of chicks each week, they should not all be kept together in one brooder. We find that we can put about three consecutive weeks' hatches together before starting a new brooder box. This is necessary because the little ones require a higher temperature than the big guys and because the bigger chicks will trample the babies, pick at them, and in general be more active, preventing the younger ones from getting as much rest as they need.

For the first two years we raised chicks, we kept them in boxes in the house. Then we purchased a proper brooder and installed it in the garage. But people remember the earlier years, and we are still known as "the people with the chickens in their living room." Even now they will walk into the house, look around, and say, "Don't you have chickens anymore?"

12
Chickens for Meat

The first rule to remember if you plan on raising chickens for meat is never to name a bird you intend to eat! Either you won't be able to "do it" when the time comes, or that beautiful roast chicken will sit on the table while you and the kids sit around with tears in your eyes. If you must name your future meal, call it Colonel Sanders or Cacciatore. Above all, try to take a lighthearted attitude toward the whole matter. It's the only way you'll ever be able to do your own butchering and keep your sanity.

If you are raising chickens specifically for meat, be sure to get a suitable breed. Leghorns, for instance, will be nothing but tough and stringy by the time there's enough meat on them to make a meal. We discuss types of birds to raise for the table in Chapter 15, "Starting Your Flock."

Information on economical commercial methods of raising broiler flocks is available from local cooperative extension service offices. However, raising chickens in your backyard to fill the freezer is not a particularly economical enterprise. As we mentioned, feed isn't cheap. Besides, you could never compete with the efficiency of the chicken industry with a small flock roaming the backyard. But you will notice the difference in taste, and you will know exactly what you're eating. Remember that feeding your meat birds with table scraps, overripe fruit, salad greens, etc., as well as letting them forage for bugs and weeds, is what makes them taste so exceptionally homegrown good, with a flavor that cannot be matched by a commercial mass-production operation.

Nonetheless, we have found that if future fryers aren't given high-protein feeds as they grow, the results will be most disappointing. Chicks fed with a commercially prepared high-protein mixture grow larger and faster. They are healthier and less susceptible to disease, due to the vitamin and mineral supplements in the feed.

If you choose to use a medicated feed, observe the directions on the label for withdrawal of that type of feed prior to slaughter. That way you won't get any chicken medications on your dinner plate.

The younger the chickens are when butchered, the more tender they will be. A chicken can still be used for frying up to about six months of age, and from six months to about a year it should be roasted in a slow oven. From then on it's strictly stew meat. It is general commercial practice to butcher chickens between 8 and 16 weeks of age. Because our chickens run free and burn up a lot of energy, we prefer to wait about 16 to 22 weeks, when they are nice and plump. Of course, they're eating more during that time, but they're growing, too. If we feed them lots of scraps and leftovers in addition to their regular feed, the extra growing time isn't too expensive. We haven't noticed any loss in tenderness up to that time either, unless the chickens have really been running all over the place. We try to get them to eat a lot and grow fast, and don't let them run around *too* much. While the chicken we eat is not always as "tender" as that sold in the stores, we regard our chickens as nice and firm and full of flavor, and we have come to feel that store-bought chicken is mushy and tasteless. It all depends on your taste and on the condition of your teeth. Try a few at different ages and see which you prefer. If you're in doubt about the age of the chicken you plan to butcher, check the breastbone—the more flexible the breastbone, the more tender the meat will be.

Incidentally, the meat in homemade chickens is darker due to their greater activity. The color of the meat, or muscle, has to do with the amount of activity the bird has been allowed, and in banties even the breast meat tends to be dark because they like to fly.

It is often assumed for some reason that banties don't make good meat birds. They're small, it's true, but they certainly are tasty! We never hesitate to put our surplus banty cockerels into the freezer. They are great cooked like Cornish hens or simmered in a soup. In fact, we really feel that they give a soup or stew much more flavor than the larger chickens do.

We're sometimes asked about caponizing. This is a process similar to castration whereby the reproductive organs of young cockerels are disconnected in order to channel their sexual energy into growth energy. Capons grow several pounds heavier than their brethren the same age and are said to have better meat. They also tend to have a calmer disposition and usually crow less often. Larger breeds—Rocks, Reds, and hybrid crosses—are generally used for caponizing, although with the new improved heavy strains available now, such as Hubbards, caponizing is no longer practiced commercially to as great an extent as in former years. We have never tried caponizing, for two reasons. First, unless you are very experienced at it, you could kill the bird; even expert caponizers incur some loss, though it's a small percentage. Second, if you mildly botch the job and the bird lives (such a bird is aptly called a slip), you can have all sorts of medical and social problems with him. But don't let us scare you off. Once you get the hang of it, apparently it isn't very difficult. We know someone who hired herself out as an expert caponizer after having only seen someone caponize a few cockerels, and she didn't lose a single bird. If you're interested in learning more about it, the USDA puts out a pamphlet called *Caponizing Chickens,* and the book *Raising Poultry the Modern Way* contains a clear description of the operation. Since there are different methods of caponizing, it would be best to read up on the subject before purchasing anything.

If you want to raise chickens for meat but don't feel you want to do the butchering yourself, slaughtering services can sometimes be found through the yellow pages of the phone book or the classified section of your local newspaper.

BUTCHERING

Now let's get down to the nitty-gritty. (If you tend to be squeamish about these things, perhaps at this point you would rather skip to the next chapter, on *showing* chickens!) Our method of butchering is something we worked out and may not conform to advice you hear elsewhere, so do whatever you think is best. We want to give you some idea of what's involved and to show you that it doesn't have to be as complicated as some descriptions make it.

The first thing we do in preparing to butcher chickens is to take them off of feed for at least 12 hours. A crop full of sour grain bursting during the cleaning process does nothing to improve your appetite for chicken, and it's difficult to clean all those little pieces of grain from the body cavity once they get scattered around. We leave water for them, however, so that they won't begin to dehydrate.

There are several ways to kill a chicken but most are a little too personal for us, as we prefer to remain at least an ax-handle away. Hold the chicken by the legs, lay its head on a chopping block, and chop off the head with a good sharp ax. The chickens usually will hold nice and still—they tend to become very philosophical about their fate when you have them by both legs, and they don't discover you're up to something until they're in two pieces. Then hold the chicken upside down for a while to let it bleed. If the flapping around bothers you, tie a noose around the feet and hang the bird for a few minutes to let it drain. If you let go of the chicken, it will thrash wildly around on the ground for several minutes. It doesn't really run around with its head cut off as the proverb says, but it certainly makes an entertaining attempt. We like to do about four chickens at a time, which takes about an hour of plucking if the chickens aren't moulting and far too long if they are. In case they do happen to be moulting when butchering day comes around, we prefer to put it off a few weeks until the feathers are all in and are firm enough to pick with ease.

While you are busy with the butchering, have a large kettle of water coming to a boil on the stove. Dip one chicken in the hot water, holding it by the feet and using the legs to push it under (you'll see how it works when you try it). Hold it under for a few seconds, but not too long as the skin will cook and will tear when you try to pull the feathers out. Then quickly dip the chicken in a sink full of cold tap water, being careful not to drip the boiling water down your front or all over the floor on your way to the sink. What you've just done is opened the pores so that the feathers will release easily and then cooled off the chicken so the skin won't cook. Now start stripping off the feathers as fast as you can, pulling them in the direction they grow so the skin won't tear. If they don't come off easily, you didn't leave the bird in the hot water long enough, so do it again. After a while you'll know how long to dip it. The reason for not tearing the skin is purely aesthetic, so if that happens, don't throw the chicken out—smother it in mushrooms.

We like to pluck the wings first because the bird stiffens quickly, and it becomes harder to clean the feathers out from its wingpits. After the feathers have been removed, tweeze the small pinfeathers between a paring knife and your thumb. When you get one chicken done, rinse off any loose feathers that may be sticking, pat with a towel to start it drying, set it aside, and go on to the next.

When all four are plucked, go back to the first and pass it over a flame to singe off the hairlike things that stick up after the bird has dried a bit. Don't hold it too close to the flame— you don't want to roast it yet. Cut off the legs where the shank

Cutting out the oil gland.

joins the drumstick, and cut the stub of the neck back to clean meat. Cut off the little bump on the tail, making sure to get all the yellow stuff around it, too. This is the oil gland that the chicken uses to oil its feathers, and we hear it tastes terrible.

With the chicken on its back, and using a small, very sharp knife, make an incision just forward of the vent, and slit the skin to the breastbone. Don't cut very deeply as you don't want to puncture the intestine. Now, entering through this slit, work your hand all around the inside cavity of the bird between the body wall and the organs. When you have loosened the organs sufficiently, reach in as far as you can and pull the innards gently toward you. If you're lucky, almost everything will come out in one neat bundle. Cut around the vent to release the organs completely, and separate out the gizzard, liver, and heart, if you want to save them.

We are not overly fond of heart and gizzard meat but have found that if it's ground up in a meat chopper it makes great pizzas and tacos. Cleaning the gizzard is a little tricky if you've never seen one whole. The gizzard is roundish and closed up something like a clam around an inner sac. The sac has a tough lining and is filled with little stones and sometimes glass chips, nails, and other weird junk. You have to slice the gizzard halfway around and take out the inside lining. If you've done a good job slicing through the outer part (the part you want to save), you won't cut into the inner sac, and it will just peel away with the smelly stuff still inside of it. But if you cut all the way through, you may want to rinse out the pebbles and junk before you peel away the lining.

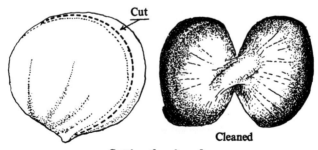

Cutting the gizzard.

The liver needs some cleaning, too. It has a little green bile sac attached to it. Try to cut it off without breaking it or the liver will take on a bitter taste. Chicken livers are a real treat, so save them up and do something great with them.

Sometimes the heart will be left way up inside the cavity. If so, pull it out. Although it is unnecessary, some people like to remove the lungs, too; these are the squishy things beyond the heart. If you're doing a rooster, you'll have to remove the testicles. Oddly enough, these two white oval objects are way up inside the bird, about in the middle of the back. If it's a hen you're cleaning, there may be a cluster of small egg yolks about in the same place. Now turn the bird on its breast and slit the neck skin a few inches, from the cut opening to the body cavity. Pull out the windpipe and the crop, if they didn't come out with the other organs, cut off the neck—and you're done!

If you had trouble visualizing all this, don't despair: we had trouble too, until we tried it. Once all the feathers are off, you'll recognize the chicken as very much like something you'd get at the market, and it will be fairly obvious what to do. For your first attempt, you might have a friend read this description to you as you go along. It's essential to work fairly rapidly to get the chickens into the refrigerator as soon as possible. Leaving warm meat at room temperature exposes it to the risk of contamination by salmonella bacteria.

STORING THE MEAT

To prepare the chickens for storing, rinse them in cold water inside and out, drain, pat dry, and wrap them in plastic bags. Someone once showed us the trick of gathering up the opening of the bag and sucking all the air out (using a straw, if you like) before it's tied shut. If there's no hole in the bag, this should help preserve the meat. Put the wrapped chickens in the refrigerator for 24 to 48 hours so that rigor mortis can run its course and allow the meat to become soft again. Then you can cook up the chickens to eat or put them in the freezer. If you don't allow this aging period, the meat is likely to be a little tough. If you use special freezer bags and have a freezer that

107

maintains a temperature of -10° F., you can keep the chickens in it for up to a year.

If freezer space is a problem, you might want to cut the chickens into pieces. Spend some time looking at chicken pieces at the meat counter when you go shopping, and you will have a pretty good idea how to go about it. The USDA puts out a pamphlet on canning poultry and another on freezing it (see the Appendix for the address). The latter contains photos showing how to cut up a fryer.

We probably needn't warn you against giving chicken bones to your dog or cat. But you might not have thought of this: if you feed raw chicken organs or raw meat to your pets, you may very well be giving them a taste for it, and sometime when they get a craving, they may not wait for you to do the butchering. We recommend cooking any of the meat fed to pets. It's a bit of a hassle but worth it in the long run.

You will find that butchering chickens is a real experience, and it will give you a new appreciation for the meat you eat. Remember, all that meat hermetically sealed in neat plastic packages at the supermarket was once living animals, and somewhere somebody is making his living spilling their blood all day long for you. You'll have to come to terms with this on your own. We have friends who butchered their chickens one day and became vegetarians the next.

13
Chickens for Show

Raising standard-bred chickens for show can be an interesting and rewarding hobby. Our purpose in this brief chapter is to convince you that showing and breeding for show are not simple and that it is important for you to get all the help you can in understanding the subtleties before you actually start. You can avoid disappointment and frustration by joining one or more organizations, by visiting shows, and by reading widely. See the Appendix to find where publications mentioned in this chapter may be obtained, and also where to apply for membership in some organizations.

There is a considerable number of general poultry associations, as well as specialized organizations for nearly every breed. If you already know what kind of birds you want to raise, you can join a group that specializes in the breed you like. Most of these are national organizations, so you might want to join a local general club as well. By attending local meetings and shows, you will get to know other people who are interested in showing chickens. They can help you get started by telling you where good show stock can be obtained and by answering many of your questions on the special care show birds need. Many poultry organizations put out yearbooks containing pertinent information and listing breeders of show quality birds. Membership in the American Bantam Association, for one, is inexpensive and entitles you to quarterly bantam culture course lessons. The information given can often be applied to large breeds as well.

You might want to subscribe to the *Poultry Press,* which reports on many of the competitions around the country and sometimes contains useful and interesting articles on raising and caring for show chickens. You can also find out about many of the different organizations by reading this periodical.

Selecting, Fitting, and Showing Poultry, by Julius E. Nordby, contains some good tips on preparing birds for show, including how to give a chicken a bath. This helpful book is now out of print but may be available through your local library.

Above all, acquire a copy of the American Poultry Association's *Standard of Perfection.* The *Standard* contains descriptions of all of the recognized breeds of chickens and has a great many pictures to help acquaint you with what they should look like. The birds you will want for show should look as much as possible like the birds described in the *Standard.* The American Bantam Association has also put out a book, the *Bantam Standard.* For those who raise bantams, this book makes a nice supplement to the A.P.A. *Standard.* It is clear, well organized, and has a lot of nice pictures.

A standard-bred frizzled Sultan.

It is difficult, though, to get a really good idea of what a bird should look like just from reading a book. A good way to find out what the "ideal" chicken looks like is to attend fairs and shows. Compare the winning birds with those placing second and third, and compare them all with the pictures in your *Standard*. (Always take it with you when you intend to look at chickens.) Try to determine why the judges ranked the birds as they did. One respected and well-known judge of our acquaintance always carries his *Standard* with him when he judges. He never makes an important decision without first consulting it, even though he's been judging for many years and probably has most of the book memorized.

Once you are ready to purchase your chickens, care must be exercised in selecting them. Many people raise and sell pet quality purebreds. While these roughly fit the description of their breed and are readily identifiable as such, they are not likely to win any prizes at a show. By first acquainting yourself with birds at competitions, you should be able to make a wise choice when purchasing your own stock. You should be aware, though, that "good stock" is hard to define, because there may be considerable variations in quality even among closely related birds. Offspring of blue-ribbon stock may offer no competition whatever to their parents. And though less likely, a grand champion could hatch from mediocre stock. This is one reason it is better to buy mature stock rather than chicks or partially feathered birds. Although you'll be paying more, there's no doubt about what you're getting. It's impossible to tell by looking at a chick exactly how fine a specimen it will become as an adult. Birds change as they grow, so that until they feather fully it is difficult to determine how they will compare to the *Standard*. A chicken may not even reach its full potential as a show bird until it is nearly two years old, although generally one-year-old birds take more prizes.

Some varieties of chickens—most blues, for instance—are inherently very unstable and therefore frustrating to breed. Blues are generally a result of a black-white breeding. Their offspring, instead of being uniformly blue, may be a spectrum of shades of blue and possibly even black or white. Breeds for which the hen has one color pattern and the cock another are also difficult to breed. In order to get top-quality birds in both sexes you must breed two lines, one for male coloring and one for female coloring, almost as if you were raising two separate breeds.

Although a few of the many breeds of fancy and colorful chickens that exist today were originally found in nature and evolved spontaneously, most have been artificially created by breeders through careful crossbreeding. Chickens of any of these artificially developed breeds necessarily have varied ancestry, and in the course of ordinary breeding, throwbacks to certain odd ancestors may occur. The more recently a breed or variety has been developed, the more likely it is that throwbacks will occur. A reputable breeder will not sell chickens with which he has been experimenting or which are likely to have throwbacks, unless he tells you so. However, throwbacks can happen anytime, so it's not necessarily a sign that you have purchased impure stock.

As a breeder selects birds having the characteristics he desires, he often chooses more and more closely related ones. Even though this may result in birds of excellent show quality, they may be so highly inbred that they are difficult to raise. They may have lower disease resistance, for example, or the fertility of the cocks may be down. The game is "Win the Blue Ribbon," and these are some of the penalties of playing. You might want to purchase all of your beginning stock from one source in order to continue breeding an excellent line or you might choose to obtain stock from more than one source in order to start with unrelated birds and thereby avoid further inbreeding. This will also enable you to choose chickens with qualities which complement each other, and with judicious care in mating the birds you may substantially improve the quality of your stock. Only those offspring showing the finer qualities of both lines are retained as breeders and for show.

When buying chickens for show or show stock, look not only at the bird you intend to purchase but also at its parents, siblings, and offspring if possible. A good seller will be happy to help you make a decision, pointing out any problems each bird may have, as well as its finer qualities.

Choosing a breed and obtaining good quality stock is just the beginning for someone who is serious about raising birds for show. Show birds require specialized housing arrangements, a feeding program aimed at keeping the birds in the peak of condition, and a more carefully regulated breeding program than is necessary for the average backyard husbander. They also require special attention before and after each show. The "best" way to raise show birds varies with the breed. Tips on caring for the breed you choose can be learned through your breed specialty club and from local people experienced in raising and showing that breed.

We know a fellow who bought a chick at the local feed store, raised it up, put it in the county fair, and won first prize. But that was more luck than anything else, and it is surely not a good formula for raising consistent winners.

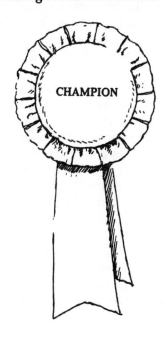

14
Advice and Solutions

By now we may have scared you out of raising chickens with all our warnings about things that can go wrong. But if you provide your flock with a clean and healthy environment, a good variety of foods, and plenty of loving care, major problems should not arise. Here are a few more tips we would like to pass on to make chicken raising easy and enjoyable.

CATCHING CHICKENS

One handy thing to know is how to catch a chicken. This should be fairly easy, once you're onto chicken psychology. If it fits into your plans, the best way to catch chickens is at night after they've gone to roost. They will be asleep when you come in and you can pick one up very easily.

If the chickens are pets and are used to being handled, it's a simple matter to reach down and pick one up anytime during the day. This is one very good reason for being on familiar terms with your flock. To catch a less friendly chicken, corner it in the coop or against the fence and grab it either by the legs or by clamping both wings down. If you have a small coop, you might chase the chicken in and shut the door so that it will have less space in which to give you the runaround. Some people use long-handled nets or hooks with which to snare the chicken's leg. We find it simpler to catch them by hand. It is best to move rapidly but deliberately, rather than to run or lunge suddenly. If the chicken gets frightened, it may fly up into the rafters, into a tree, or over the fence. It's sometimes easier to catch a chicken when you have someone help you. On the other hand, someone who is not used to chickens is often worse than useless. We usually advise novices to please stand out of the way.

A lady once told us we could have all of her banties if we would just come and catch them. We went over to get them, confident we would have no trouble. Even though we had two friends along, the chickens were so wild that we only succeeded in scattering them into the trees, into a vacant lot, and under the lady's house. After similar success on a second trip, we gave up without having caught them all. So if you don't get the knack of it at first, don't feel bad.

WING CLIPPING

If you have trouble with chickens that like to fly about and get into trouble, you might want to ground them. This can be done by cutting a few flight feathers of only one wing with a pair of scissors. It does no real harm to the chicken (although to hear some of them squawk, you would think it was killing them). The idea is to upset the bird's balance enough so that it can't fly very high. The feathers will come back eventually, so be sure to check and reclip them, especially after the moult.

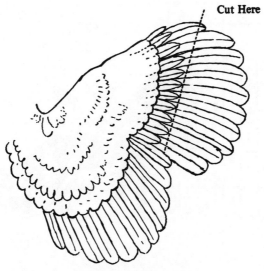

Cut Here

Where to clip the wing.

115

There are some disadvantages to wing clipping. It does spoil the appearance of the bird, and this bothers some people. If you expect to show the bird, it will be disqualified if the feathers are cut. You should also consider whether or not you'll be letting the chickens out into an open area, like a pasture or orchard, where they might be easy prey for stray cats or dogs. If the wings are clipped, they may not be able to escape.

MARAUDERS

Once upon a time a stray cat lived in the fields behind our house. Each spring she would slip over our fence to find food for her kittens, and our little chicks disappeared one by one. If you have a mysterious marauder pillaging your flocks, you might want to set a trap to catch it. Havahart (whose address is in the Appendix) makes traps that will not harm the animal; if the midnight skulker turns out to be your neighbor's pet, you

will not only have positive proof who the offender was, but you will also be able to avoid a possible feud by returning the animal unharmed. The culprit might be anything from a weasel or skunk to a coon or coyote however, and you may need professional help. Many counties provide a trapping service, and if you have persistent problems they will send someone out to trap the animal for you free of charge.

Sooner or later you will almost certainly have an infestation of rats or mice in your coop, robbing your grains. The fastest and surest method of exterminating them is to feed them poison grain, which can be purchased at a feed store or from your agricultural extension service. Follow the precautions on the label so you don't poison your flock. Better yet, set out rat traps. Although slower and more hassle, traps provide a safe extermination method if you're worried about poisoning kids or pets with treated grains.

Incidentally, if you should ever have a problem with a neighbor's dog, be aware of your legal rights. These may vary with the locality, but nowhere need you put up with dogs marauding your flocks, even if there is no specific leash law. Hopefully, you can settle the matter amicably with your neighbor. If not, call your local animal control officer. If you have seen the offending animal or can otherwise positively identify it, that is all that is needed for an agent to come out and confiscate it until the owner repays your losses. They may eventually destroy the dog if the owner refuses to meet his responsibilities. Even in that case, if the chickens were expensive enough to warrant the trouble, you might want to prosecute the uncooperative owner in small-claims court for recovery of your losses. Of course, the loss of any pet fowl is tragic, but the situation is certainly aggravated if there is considerable expense in replacing the lost birds.

HOT WEATHER

During hot summer days chickens stand around in the shade and pant with their beaks wide open and their wings held away from their bodies. Since they don't perspire, this is their

117

Hot chicken.

method of keeping cool. An ample supply of drinking water is especially important in such weather. If the temperature is very high, spray the area and coop roof with a hose or set a sprinkler out to create cooling through evaporation. When it's exceptionally hot and dry we sometimes spray the chickens themselves with a fine mist. It is important to remember that chickens cannot tolerate extreme heat and may die from it. On hot days be sure to check your flock periodically to see how it is doing.

FROSTBITE

Our friends in colder climates tell us that frostbite is a hazard to chickens during the winter. Especially vulnerable are the combs and wattles, which will redden in color and become swollen if they have been affected and may eventually die back and fall off. If you suspect your chickens have been frostbitten, treat as you would any case of frostbite—by rubbing affected parts with snow or cold water. Frostbitten combs and wattles are extremely painful once they have thawed. The birds may become listless and stop eating, and amputation of the combs and wattles may be in order. In fact, many people up north make a practice of removing the combs and wattles from young chicks to prevent the possibility of frostbite later on. In cold areas, an insulated coop with well-placed electric light bulbs will help keep the flock from becoming uncomfortably cold.

BANDING

Chickens are sometimes banded to keep track of where they came from or what age they are. This is done by putting a commercially made coil, coded by color or by number, around the chicken's shank. These bands can usually be purchased at feed

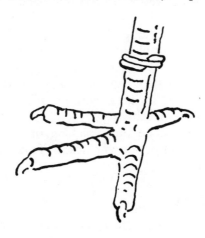

Expandable banding spiral.

stores and come in different types for different size chickens. If you band your chickens, watch to make sure that the shank doesn't expand around the band, as this will cause swelling and infection. Keep in mind that it is especially a problem with growing birds, so increase the band size as the bird gets larger.

FEATHER LOSS

People who raise chickens for the first time are sometimes alarmed by the moult, which usually occurs each autumn when the chickens lose their feathers and get new ones. It doesn't happen to all the chickens at once, and most of the time it happens so gradually that it's hardly noticeable, but sometimes a chicken may look almost bare. During the moult, make sure the birds are getting a good diet with plenty of protein to help their bodies build new feathers.

Sometimes feather loss occurs in the spring in the form of bare patches across a hen's back or on her head. This is caused by the rooster holding on with his claws and beak during breeding and is usually nothing to worry about. But if the cock has clawed through the skin on a hen's back, she should be removed from the flock until she is completely healed. This rarely happens unless there are too few hens per cock or the birds are closely confined.

Another cause of feather loss is a type of mite, appropriately known as the depluming mite, which burrows into the chicken's skin. The chicken scratches and picks at its feathers and sometimes pulls them out. Keeping the coop clean and mite-free, as described in the section on mites and lice in this chapter, will help prevent this.

Feather loss can also be due to picking, or the pulling out of one chicken's feathers by another chicken. This is often the first sign of cannibalism.

CANNIBALISM

Bored or overcrowded chickens sometimes resort to cannibalism as an interesting diversion. This has dire consequences

120

both for the rest of the flock and for the person who is trying to raise them. It is extremely provoking to go out to the barnyard and find that Tuesday's dinner has eaten Wednesday's or that your red-ribbon bird has devoured your blue-ribbon bird. For most backyard husbanders, cannibalism usually occurs in young birds, often due to too much light or heat in the brooder. In the case of both young and older flocks, nutritional deficiencies or inadequate watering and feeding space may also be contributing factors.

Bored chicks often start by picking each other's toes (or even their own). Older birds may start picking at the base of the tail or near the vent. Should a bird get caught in a fence or otherwise trapped, the other chickens may mercilessly pick it until it is plucked bare and eaten alive. An injury of any sort provides an occasion for picking to start. The chickens may finish off one unfortunate bird and nonchalantly go on to eat others. Whenever a bird has been injured in any way, move it into isolation until the wound has healed completely. Sometimes there is a ringleader or one persistent picker. Removing it from the flock may take care of the whole problem.

Preventing overcrowding is essential. Be especially sure to provide chicks with plenty of room in which to move around. They grow with astonishing rapidity—just like popcorn! So plan ahead. Gradually increase the size of their available space as the chicks grow. Once they reach maturity, they should be provided with adequate space to run around and to scratch and dust in, as described in Chapters 4 and 5 on the coop and run. Also be sure that all birds can get to the feed and water.

Boredom is less likely to occur if chickens always have a variety of feeds to peck at. Chicks on a high-protein diet will be less likely to develop cannibalism, and inadequate protein might even cause cannibalism in an adult flock. Feeding alfalfa or oats to a flock in which cannibalism is starting sometimes helps get the problem under control.

Caged birds or chicks in a brooder might enjoy having a toy of some sort to play with. For instance, they like to peck at shiny objects hanging from the ceiling or attached to the wall. Shredded rags suspended in the cage provide something for them to tug at, but make sure there aren't a lot of loose threads they could choke on. Birds enjoy reaching for and eating suspended leafy greens.

If cannibalism appears to be starting in your brooder, replace the light bulb with a red one and keep the brooder away from direct sunlight. A red light neutralizes the red color of blood, making it difficult to notice. There are antipicking preparations which are red and taste awful (we hear), available at feed stores. The compound is applied to any open wounds. Once a chicken has had a taste of it, it is supposed to lose interest in pursuing cannibalistic activities. In a pinch, you might try spreading tree sealer or roofing tar thinly over the wound. There are also eye guards available, called specs, that look like sunglasses and are really comical. They are sometimes used to stop picking, though we've only seen them used once. Commercial chicken raisers often deal with cannibalism by debeaking (clipping the beaks). We think this makes the chickens look ugly, and we doubt you would want to do it.

Once cannibalism has gotten started, it can be tricky to stop. If the conditions which caused the problem in the first place aren't changed, then nothing short of debeaking or individual caging will help. Early prevention by proper care is the best way to deal with this problem.

WORMS

Like cats and dogs, chickens have the tendency to pick up infestations of worms in the digestive tract. Chickens may get many varieties. Two types are familiar to dog and cat owners: roundworms and tapeworms.

Wild birds stopping in for a snack often start the cycle by leaving a few worm eggs with their droppings before they fly away. Some types of worms are picked up by the chickens directly from these droppings. Others must first be picked up from the bird droppings by earthworms, grasshoppers, and various insects. They in turn are eaten by chickens, who thereby inherit the problem. One such type of worm is particularly prevalent in the southern states, so poultry raisers in those areas might be a little cautious about allowing chickens to run loose to forage for bugs. Thus, although we are enthusiastic about allowing chickens as much free range as possible, this does have its disadvantages.

Once the first worms have been picked up by a chicken, the problem rapidly intensifies. The worms lay a large number of eggs, which are expelled from the chicken in its droppings and may eventually be picked up by another chicken or even the same chicken. Reduce the opportunity for these worms to spread by keeping the coop and run clean and building a droppings pit under the perches where most of the droppings collect and the chickens can't get into them.

Worms are not a major problem to small flocks whose owners are conscientious about cleanliness, and we caution you against indiscriminate use of worming preparations. However, when worm problems do develop the main concern is usually that afflicted chickens are more prone to contracting diseases due to lowered resistance. If a bird doesn't lay as well as it should, seems to be weak, has runny droppings, loses weight (or in the case of a young bird, doesn't gain as rapidly as you would expect), but otherwise seems healthy enough, then worms can reasonably be suspected as a possible cause.

Different wormers are required for different types of worms, but it is not always a simple matter to determine what kind of worms, if any, a chicken has. Some preparations contain multiple wormers. Should you decide to worm your birds, try a piperazine preparation for roundworms first, as this is a fairly safe wormer (if used according to directions) and hopefully it will do the trick. We find that taking away the chicken's feed the night before worming increases the wormer's effectiveness. Worm all chickens in one flock at the same time.

Before worming a bird, be sure that you have ruled out any diseases that might possibly cause the symptoms you are ascribing to worms. We have known people to kill birds by withholding feed and worming them, when in fact the birds were sick and required another type of medical treatment. And by all means be careful to follow the dosage directions on the label. We know of a case in which a prize-winning show bird died of an overdose of wormer administered by its owner who wanted to be absolutely sure he finished off those pesky worms.

MITES AND LICE

Body parasites can be a real problem for chickens. They crawl all over the head and body, biting and chewing and sucking blood until the poor chicken is driven to distraction. These parasites can cause a good deal of blood loss, lowering the bird's resistance to disease. A setting hen provides an ideal stationary home for them, and they may so totally infest her body that they will cause her death. Neither are mites and lice a pleasure to the person whose hand and arm are crawling with the things after handling a bird or equipment in the coop.

Chickens confined completely by a coop and run usually won't get mites or lice unless an affected chicken is brought in, and then the vermin will spread through the whole flock. When wild birds and rodents can get in with the chickens, they sometimes leave body parasites with the flock.

There are all sorts of mites and lice, and they affect various parts of a bird's body. Some kinds of mites spend the day on the perches and in the cracks of the coop but crawl onto the chickens at night when they go to roost. Others live perpetually on the birds' bodies. Mites are minute specks that are difficult to see, but they can sometimes be observed by looking closely in the fluff between the feathers on the underside of a chicken, especially around the vent. They may be either red or light brown. If you see little things crawling around in the litter or nesting boxes, they are probably mites. Lice are brownish yellow in color and are generally larger and thus easier to see than mites. They spend their entire lives on the chicken's body. Their eggs stick to the feathers in clumps and look something like gray rice.

If your chickens are exposed to lice and mites, you should check them occasionally and eliminate the vermin before they get out of hand. Go out at night and examine one or two of the

One type of chicken louse.

chickens. You won't have to check them all—if one has vermin, they all will. Avoid getting these parasites on your clothing and body. Should you fail, put the clothes in the washer and yourself in the shower, immediately.

Rather than letting vermin get into the flock and then eliminating them, it is better for the chickens, and easier for you, to take preventive measures. There are a number of preparations available at feed stores and from poultry medication supply outlets (such as those advertising in *Poultry Press*) that will prevent this problem. These are usually sprayed around the inside of the coop or painted on the perches with a brush, and provide extended control over a period of time. Alternate preparations to keep the vermin from becoming immune to one type. Old-time chicken raisers highly recommend brushing common crankcase oil on perches and into cracks of the coop as a mite and lice preventive.

Dust baths help eliminate body parasites, so the chickens should be able to dust when they want to. If they don't have a natural dusting place, it's a good idea to provide them with some sort of dust bin of soft dry dirt. A little rotenone and sulfur (sold at nurseries as an insecticide for plants) mixed with the dirt will provide extra protection.

125

Scaly leg mites are another parasite that can be brought in by wild birds. These pests cause the scales on the shanks of the chicken to stick out and sometimes to flake off. They may make the bird do the goose step like a Prussian soldier and can eventually cripple it. Get rid of the mites by dipping the chicken's feet and shanks in a mixture of two parts oil to one part kerosene. Two or three dippings, about two weeks apart, may be necessary before the mites are entirely eliminated. Again, keep the poultry yard clean to help prevent this problem. For a small flock, clean the shanks and rub them with carbolated petroleum jelly (Vaseline).

EGG EATING

Many chicken raisers have to deal with egg eating at one time or another. You will know you have this problem if you find empty shells in the nest and yolk smeared around in the litter or on other eggs. If this happens, make sure the chickens are getting enough calcium. Put out a supply of oyster shells; if the chickens really go for it, calcium deficiency was probably the trouble. To make sure they have plenty of calcium, put shells in their feed each day, or better yet, leave a containerful where they can get to it anytime.

Egg eating can get started when a hen accidentally breaks an egg in the nest, eats it, and finds out how good it is. Usually though, an egg breaks because the shell was too thin, and this again is a result of calcium deficiency. Egg eating can also start when unground eggshells are thrown out for the chickens. It's a great idea to recycle eggshells, but they should always be mashed or ground in the blender. Boredom sometimes leads to egg eating, so try to let the chickens out where they can scratch around a lot and have plenty to do. Frequent collecting of eggs during the day removes temptation; having the nests in a darkened location usually helps discourage egg eaters; and leaving a stone egg in the nest should certainly deter even the most persistent offender. If you can isolate the guilty hen, remove her for a while to a new place and give her lots of good things to eat until she has forgotten about eating eggs. Roosters will also eat eggs, so it's not always the hens you should suspect. To identify the culprit, look for the one standing around with egg on its face. Egg eating can spread through a flock once the others catch on to what they've been missing, so if you see it starting, stop it while you can. We have occasionally had cases of egg eating among our chickens, and all have been stopped by following the above procedures. But should you get an inveterate egg eater, it would be best to remove it permanently from the flock before it teaches its bad habits to the others.

EGG BINDING

Occasionally a hen may get egg-bound, which means there is a traffic jam in her oviduct, and she may die as a result. She will be sluggish and ruffle her feathers, her abdomen will distend, and you will be able to feel eggs inside. Lubricate the oviduct with mineral oil or petroleum jelly as far in as you can reach, and try to ease the eggs down. Putting the hen under a lamp for warmth often causes the eggs to come out by themselves. Even if she's "cured" of the binding, the problem may recur if healthful conditions are not provided. A hen that has a good diet and plenty of exercise is not likely to develop this problem.

DECREASE IN LAYING

Hens stop laying now and then for various reasons, many of which are not cause for concern. Moving the hens to an unfamiliar location, changing the feed or feeding routine, and extreme or sudden changes in temperature could all cause a temporary interruption in the laying pattern. Sometimes laying will stop for a short time during the warmest part of the summer. Hens also stop laying during the moult, as they need all of their energy to make new feathers. Some breeds, or individuals within a breed, will start laying again right after the moult while others won't resume laying until spring. A lot of people don't know this, and each winter we get many requests for "a rooster that will make my hens start laying again." It is, however, irregular for laying to stop during the period of mild weather between early spring and mid-fall. Make sure the hens are getting an adequate and varied diet and plenty of water. Insufficient protein could be a cause of decreased laying. On an inadequate diet, hens cannot both put nutrients into eggs and maintain good health. Since eggs are about 65 percent water, an inadequate water supply could cause a decrease in laying. Internal or external parasites are also a possible cause. If the problem persists, watch for symptoms of disease.

SYMPTOMS AND TREATMENT OF DISEASE

Even in the healthiest of chicken flocks, a bird will die now and then. So if one day you find a dead chicken, it's no reason to become totally unglued. A rational approach would be to watch the flock for further symptoms. Of course, if your flock suddenly experiences a number of deaths at once, then you will want to find out whether or not you have an epidemic on your hands and what you should do about it.

A common recommendation is that the entire flock be destroyed or otherwise disposed of each year and the facilities and equipment totally disinfected before young replacement birds are brought in. Among other justifications, this helps to prevent spread of disease from one flock to the next over the years. However, most backyard farmers would be appalled at the thought of losing Chauntecleer or Henrietta. They might, in fact, use last year's hens to brood and rear new chicks or they might want to use one or more older birds in this year's breeding program. For such people, wholesale removal of the flock each year would be impractical, undesirable, mean, and downright out of the question. If you are such a person, this section will give you some suggestions for keeping your flock healthy.

It is sometimes advisable—and under certain circumstances, imperative—to vaccinate chickens against certain poultry diseases. This is one way to be sure of controlling a disease, though it is somewhat of a nuisance and, like any vaccination program, does carry its risks even when done correctly. Your state likely has an agricultural extension poultry specialist who can tell you if there are any diseases prevalent in the area that your chickens should be protected against. The name and address of your state's specialist can be found by calling your county agricultural or cooperative extension service office.

Disease organisms are always luring about the coop waiting for a chance to pounce on a likely victim. These organisms can be kept under control through periodic cleaning and disinfecting of the coop and equipment. Keep the birds happy and healthy by providing adequate space, fresh air, and proper feeding. It is important to eliminate possible sources of disease-causing organisms: properly dispose of any dead bird (bury it deeply or burn it); keep out wild birds and varmints such as mice and rats; and be careful about bringing in new stock. There is much to be said for maintaining a closed flock—that is, one to which additions are not made through outside sources. Anytime a new chicken is brought into the flock, there is always the possibility that it will be the source of potential problems. Whenever bringing new birds into the flock or show birds home from a competition, it's a good idea to isolate them for at least a month to see if any symptoms of disease develop. This could prevent infection and loss of an entire flock which was formerly healthy. Since a chicken may be a carrier of a disease for which it shows no symptoms, you may want to put a chicken (one that you are willing to sacrifice) into isolation with the new or returning birds. If your chicken does not develop any symptoms within about a month, then it, along with the new ones, can be returned to the flock.

As you become more and more familiar with the habits of your birds and the problems that arise in the course of time, you will be in a better and better position to be your own disease diagnostician. In fact, it is generally known among poultry raisers that the owner of a flock is often better able to diagnose and treat his sick birds than almost anyone to whom he could take them. But it does take time to learn and lots of practice, and you may make lots of mortal mistakes along the way. A person whose flock experiences little or no problems is a fortunate person, indeed, but one who is thereby less able to cope should a disease problem arise.

129

It is important to recognize symptoms of disease so that they can be treated promptly. If your flock is normally active and healthy, you will notice when something is wrong with one or more of your birds. There are many signs of illness in chickens. Birds that sit around listlessly with their feathers ruffled are usually not feeling very well. This could simply mean that they are cold (if the weather is bad), so watch for other symptoms: an unexplained drop in the amount of feed eaten or the number of eggs laid, weight loss (a sharp, meatless breastbone can be the tip-off), wheezing and sneezing, runny nose, gulping, eyes swollen shut, yellow face and comb, black comb, lameness, and runny or bloody droppings (on the ground or sticking to the feathers around the vent). If you notice any of these symptoms in one of your birds, remove it at once and watch for further developments. If several members of the flock appear affected, you might want to consult a vet or a veteran poultry raiser in your area. Be selective if you should turn to a nontrained person for advice. Old-time folk remedies abound. Some may very well be valid and effective treatments for chicken diseases. Others may not do any good at all, and in the meantime the ailing bird is going without proper help. Still others may be detrimental and actually hasten the death of your favorite feathered friend. It is not always obvious to the novice poultry raiser just what to believe.

Some people will tell you that chickens aren't worth a trip to the vet, partly because many vets know nothing about poultry problems and partly because most chickens cost less to replace than the vet would charge to treat them. Then, too, a sick chicken is likely to die anyway: unless you are really in touch with your flock, by the time you notice a chicken is ailing, it's usually too late to restore its health. But an epidemic could destroy a whole flock, and that usually *is* more costly than a vet's fee. So, it's important to find out in advance if there is a local vet that can be depended on; talk to other chicken husbanders in the area or ask at the local feed store. It is especially prudent to get professional help if a disease seems to be spreading among the flock and you are experiencing numerous losses.

Most states have one or more poultry diagnostic laboratories, and even should you find a poultry-oriented vet, he will probably send your bird to the lab. Your local agricultural or cooperative extension service office should be able to help you locate your state's lab, and if it is nearby you may be able to take the bird directly there yourself. Contact the lab before going there to find out what would be most effective for you to bring for your particular case—whether it be dead specimens, live birds exhibiting the symptoms, or whatever.

If the problem is confined to just a few chickens, you might want to try to treat the individuals yourself. Ideally, of course, you should kill any sick bird and burn or bury the carcass; it is not likely to recover anyway, and by destroying it immediately, further spread of the problem may be avoided. However, you may feel the way we do—we always want to try to save the poor creature, particularly if it is a special favorite. So if you don't want to destroy the sick bird, but cannot afford a vet or one is not immediately available, you might try to treat it yourself. Isolate the sick chicken well away from the others to prevent spread of the disease and to allow the chicken to get plenty of rest. Chickens seem to know when one among them is weakened and often pick on that one. Try to keep it warm, if possible, and especially avoid putting it in a drafty place. A light bulb placed nearby would provide some additional warmth and might hasten recovery. Give it plenty of good things to eat. We find that worms and slugs from the garden and fresh greens sometimes perk up a droopy bird. By all means provide plenty of clean, fresh water.

There are two common types of poultry medications. Tetracycline, a broad-spectrum antibiotic, is one of them. The other is a sulfa compound. Knowing when to use which (and when to use neither) is part of the knowledge gained through experience. Of the many diseases chickens can contract, several show nearly the same symptoms but are not treated with the same medications.

A word of caution is in order here: don't just give your birds antibiotics every time you think they look a little down, as overuse of antibiotics will build up tolerance in them. Then, when a real emergency arises, the drugs will have no effect. Another word of caution: if for any reason you medicate birds that you will be eating, be sure to read the label on the drug and observe the directions for withdrawal of the medication prior to slaughter.

Although trying to diagnose a disease through reading a book is often extremely confusing for the beginner, and even for the experienced poultry raiser for that matter, it is helpful to have a book on hand with which to compare the symptoms and attempt treatment. An excellent book to have around the home is *Salsbury Manual of Poultry Diseases*. It is inexpensive, clear and informative, and profusely illustrated in color. Another good reference is *The Merck Veterinary Manual*. It is a professional veterinary guide, but not so technical that amateurs cannot derive benefit from it. Both books are listed in the Appendix.

If an infectious disease does manage to take hold of a flock, sometimes the only thing that can be done is destroy the entire flock and start over. Many diseases are not transmitted through the egg, so it is occasionally possible to collect eggs from the ailing birds (if they're still laying) before disposing of them, and then hatch the eggs or have them hatched. Before the young chicks are ready to be put into the coop, the disease organisms should be eliminated; clean the coop carefully with a good disinfectant, and air it well. For some diseases, special preparations should be used to clean the coop or there may be a certain period of time to wait before new chickens can be put in. If an epidemic of some sort occurs, the vet or diagnostic lab can give you the specific details.

We cannot overemphasize the fact that strong and healthy birds, fed properly and housed in a clean dry area of adequate size, are unlikely to contract some dread disease.

15
Starting Your Flock

This chapter will bring together things to think about when purchasing chickens. It will serve somewhat as a review of various matters discussed in this book. We will attempt to help you answer these questions about starting your flock: What kind of chickens do I want? How many shall I get? Should I start with eggs, chicks, or mature stock? How much can I expect to pay? What sources are there to buy from?

WHAT KIND OF CHICKENS?

When starting a new flock, you have to decide whether you want large chickens or bantams. Bantams are normally kept as pets or for show, while the larger breeds are commonly preferred by those with a no-nonsense approach toward fresh eggs each day and fried chicken for Sunday dinner. Bantams weigh about a fourth as much as large chickens and eat correspondingly less. Though providing less meat than a larger bird, bantams are nonetheless excellent eating. Bantam hens lay rather small eggs: three are roughly equivalent to two of the size usually seen in the stores. Banty hens are valiant and tenacious setters and are often employed as natural incubators by those who raise birds. Bantams are nice in the garden because they don't eat as much of the vegetation and don't scratch quite as destructively as the larger chickens do. On the other hand, the large breeds are usually easier to confine because they don't fly as readily as the bantams do. A banty rooster's crow is high-pitched and can be ear-piercing up close while roosters of the larger breeds generally have a deeper but louder crow. There is a large assortment of breeds and varieties to choose from in either size.

Comparison of sizes of large and bantam chickens.

For the backyard raiser, personal preference plays a large part in choosing a breed. There are fancy breeds with feathered topknots like frilly bonnets, feathered feet, beards and muffs, unusual combs, extra toes, laced or spangled plumage, etc. Consult the *Standard of Perfection* to get an idea

134

what the different breeds look like, and pick one you like to
look at. It's also helpful to visit the poultry exhibit at your
county fair.

Many breeds have been developed for a specific economic
function. Generally, the heavy breeds, such as Langshans,

135

Brahmas, and Cochins, were developed as meat birds, and their egg production is not of particular economic importance; the lightweight breeds such as Leghorns, Sicilian Buttercups, and Houdans are superb layers, but their slim, trim bodies make them poor table fowl. Backyard raisers who want a good compromise bird for both meat and eggs often prefer the mediumweight dual-purpose breeds, such as Orpingtons, Reds (Rhode Island and New Hampshire), and Plymouth Rocks (white, barred, etc.). It must be remembered, though, that dual-purpose breeds will not be as efficient and therefore not as economical in either meat or egg production alone as are those strains bred specifically for one purpose or the other.

In recent years, a lot of successful experimenting has been done with hybrids, and they are now widely used commercially for meat and egg production. The Rock Cornish cross is well known for its excellent meat-producing qualities while Leghorn crosses are very successful egg layers.

One of the characteristics of a hybrid is its inability to reproduce itself. Crosses will reproduce, and very vigorously; but the offspring will not be accurate reproductions of the parent stock. It is the nature of crossbreeds to throw progeny with a wild assortment of characteristics. Commercial poultrymen don't worry about this because they generally replace their flocks annually from hatchery stock. But a backyard raiser who wants to perpetuate his flock himself might find these hybrids undesirable, as it is always necessary to go back to the original cross.

One year we got some fantastic huge white chickens in a trade, and the hens each laid a jumbo egg nearly every day. We tried to raise chicks from them so that we would have more of those wonder-hens, but instead we got a flock of chickens of the most varied assortment of sizes and colors. Apparently our whites were some type of crossbreed. To raise hybrids like these, you would have to find out how the cross was made and acquire the chickens you need in order to do your own crossing. A simpler way to be certain to get exactly the strain you want is to get the chicks from the hatchery each time you want to renew your stock. If you intend to raise your own chicks, however, you may wish to avoid hybrids and even sacrifice a little on meat and egg production in order to get a type that breeds true.

If you live in an area where weather extremes are likely, adaptability to climate is an important consideration. The more heavily feathered breeds, such as Brahmas, Orpingtons, and Cochins, hold up well in the colder areas and often lay better in cold weather than do the lightly feathered breeds. But they tend to go broody more quickly as the weather warms, so you might want to have a mixture of breeds in order to get eggs over a longer period. Other breeds that adapt fairly well to cold (but which don't tend to brood as readily) are Rocks, Reds, and Leghorns. Leghorns are well suited to the very warm areas as well. Check with your state agricultural extension poultry man or with feed stores to see what breeds are most popular and successful locally.

Another consideration in choosing a breed is the disposition of the birds. In closely confined areas, the calmer, more sedate breeds will fare better. In our experience, these would include Silkies, Cochins, and Cornish, but there are many others. Your own temperament may be a factor also. If your backyard flock serves as your tranquilizer, high-strung flighty breeds, such as Sebrights and Buttercups, would not provide the same calm atmosphere as the more sedate breeds.

We want to emphasize that the breeds named above are illustrative examples and do not by any means constitute an exhaustive list. Often several breeds will suit any one purpose with an equal degree of satisfaction, and you needn't feel you must limit your choice to one we have named.

HOW MANY?

Chickens are social animals, so never get just one—it will get lonesome. Two will keep each other company. Three are even better, because if something happens to one, the remaining two will still have each other. A good way to start out is with one cock and two hens. After three chickens, it's a matter of the amount of space you have and on why you want chickens. For meat, decide how many you can eat in a year, and get a few extra in case you lose some. For eggs, remember that backyard chickens average about one egg every two days or so and that three banty eggs are roughly equivalent to two regular-size eggs. It you want fertile eggs, see our comments in Chapter 7, "Roosters," on how many cocks would be appropriate for your size flock.

When starting a flock from eggs, allow some extra for any that may not hatch, and when starting with chicks, allow for some that may not live to maturity. For a wide margin of safety, we like to set twice as many eggs as we want to hatch, and plan to hatch twice the number of chicks we expect will reach maturity. So if we want 25 fryers to provide us with meat and 25 hens for laying, we'll set 200 eggs, expect about 100 chicks, and plan on 50 mature birds. Of course, we often wind up with many more chickens than we need, but too many is better than too few, and friends are always willing to come over for a barbeque to help use up the surplus.

EGGS, CHICKS, OR CHICKENS?

Besides deciding what breed and how many, you must decide whether to start with eggs, chicks, or chickens. You may want to begin with eggs if you are able to purchase hatching eggs of the breed you choose, have access to an incubator, and are willing to try your luck with it. Before you decide to start this way, be sure you have read Chapter 10 on incubating so that you know what's involved. If you follow the instructions and don't have any accidents, you should be relatively successful; however, because of the many factors involved—vitality of parent stock, age of eggs, how carefully the incubation instructions are followed, etc.—the hatch will seldom come close to 100 percent.

Don't buy eggs for hatching from a grocery store. They are almost never fertile and have been refrigerated besides, so they surely won't hatch. Buy eggs that are sold specifically for hatching. Even though eggs sold for hatching cost more than eating eggs, they nonetheless will not be guaranteed to hatch! There are too many variables not under the egg seller's control. However, they should be guaranteed to be of the breed they were sold as and to have been stored properly prior to sale.

You may want to start your flock with chicks and avoid the frailties of incubating. If you're buying chicks from a hatchery or feed store, you will have a choice of getting those that are sexed or straight-run. Chicks of several hybrid strains (and of a few pure breeds) can be sexed by clearly visible characteristics such as color or comb type. Most purebred chicks, however, would have to be sexed by examination of the vent. It is extremely difficult to vent-sex very young chicks with any degree of accuracy, but there are professional sexers who have been trained to look for very subtle differences between pullets and cockerels. Still, even the highly skilled professionals employed by hatcheries can't be more than about 95 percent accurate. Furthermore, they must see the chicks within their first 24 hours of life, because after that "they all look alike," as a sexer once told us. It is difficult to determine their sex again for sure until they are a few weeks old, and then it is done by less mysterious means—namely, by observing the developing secondary sexual characteristics.

Whether you buy sexed or straight-run chicks depends on your purpose in raising them. If you want an all-purpose flock, straight-run will provide about a 50-50 mixture of pullets for laying and cockerels for fryers. If for any reason you do not want roosters, it is best to try to purchase sexed pullets. But they will be more expensive than straight-run, and remember about five percent usually turn out to be cockerels anyway. If you want a batch of chicks to raise for meat, then cockerels of a medium to heavy breed make a good investment, even though they, too, are usually slightly higher in price than straight-run. Cockerels grow bigger faster than pullets of the same breed.

Don't be taken in by so-called fantastic bargains on light-weight cockerels. When a hatchery gets a large order for pullets, they may have a surplus of cockerels which they must destroy. If you happen along at the right time, you can often get them for a good price. Occasionally feed stores acquire these chicks and give them to their customers with each purchase of feed. But the birds are likely to be a lightweight breed neither suitable for commercial meat production nor particularly desirable for home use. In the long run you will find that your initial saving is more than lost in feeding the birds, especially for the small quantity and poor quality of meat you'll get.

All breeds are not always available from sources that provide a sexing service, so you may have to settle for straight-run from the typical farmer, backyard hobbyist, or small breeder. Chicks purchased from individuals will almost always be straight-run because sexing is a very specialized field requiring training and a good deal of practice, and it is rare when a private breeder knows much about it. Do not expect the person from whom you purchase your chicks to trade pullets for your cockerels after the chicks have grown large enough to distinguish. A much greater number of hens than cocks is needed in breeding chickens, and nearly everyone who raises chickens has the problem of too many roosters. Plan to deal with this on your own, either by buying only pullets when possible or by finding homes or recipes for your surplus cockerels.

The advantages of starting with chicks rather than mature birds are that the chicks get to know you and more readily become pets, they are cheaper than mature birds, and they are less likely to carry diseases. There are disadvantages too: they are some trouble and require special care to get them through the critical growing stage (see Chapter 11, "The Care and Feeding of Chicks"). A certain percentage of mortality must be expected with chicks, whereas mature birds have already passed through the stress-filled maturation period and are therefore less likely to die. Moreover, when you buy chicks you can't really tell what the grown birds will look like. This is especially important if you plan to show, though if you just want a lot of laying hens or meat birds, it doesn't matter how closely they conform to the *Standard*. Instead of choosing between day-old chicks and mature chickens, a nice compromise is started chicks, if you can find them in the breed you want. These are chicks that are partially grown. The more growing stages they've passed through, the easier they will be for you to raise.

When purchasing mature stock remember that a hen's egg laying and cock's virility will decline with age and that, although they may live much longer, they are generally considered "old" at four or five years. Novices sometimes have trouble determining the age of mature birds. One way to get an idea of the age of the bird is to look at its shanks; a young chicken will have very smooth shanks while an older bird's will be larger and rougher. Check the breastbone, too; a young chicken will have a flexible breastbone while an older bird's breastbone will be more rigid. We've heard of several cases of people thinking they got a real bargain on laying hens only to find that somebody peddled them a whole batch of worn-out hens from an eggery. (In fact, we know of a young fellow who specializes in such sales.) In Chapter 8, "Chickens for Eggs," we explained how to tell if a hen is laying. If a hen does not show characteristics of a layer, but indications are that she is no longer a pullet, don't let anyone con you with the line that she hasn't started

Cock and hen.

laying yet. It may very well be true, of course, but if so, it will be true forever.

When buying mature birds, you should be able to identify them by sex. The comb and wattles of a cock are usually larger and brighter than the hen's. In most breeds, the hackle (neck) and saddle (lower back) feathers of a cock are pointed at the ends while the female's are more rounded. The cock will usually have a larger, more sweeping tail. Cocks have spurs that grow longer with age while a hen's spurs will be tiny if she has them at all.

COST

There are several factors that determine the initial cost of a chicken. The price you pay will depend a lot on the type you buy. Some breeds are harder to find, tricky to raise, or in greater demand, and these will be more expensive. The closer to maturity a bird is, the more investment the breeder has in it, in time as well as money, so the more he must charge for it. The season may also have some bearing on prices. Chickens bought in the spring will often be more expensive than those purchased in autumn because the breeder has had to feed them through the unproductive winter season. Breeders like to reduce their flocks in the fall, and it's often bargain time for buyers who don't mind winter feeding. For this very reason, laying hens will be more difficult to find in the spring. People often don't want to purchase hens until the laying season starts, and competition for those available in spring is much greater. Very fine show birds are usually priced by appearance more than by season: the closer the bird conforms to the *Standard of Perfection,* the higher the asking price.

We would like to quote specific prices to give you an idea of what to expect, but this is impractical because prices vary with such things as the locale, the season, the breed, the age, and the cost of feed. The best way to get an idea of what to expect to pay in your area is to visit several sources and compare their prices.

Occasionally you will find chickens going for substantially

less than the prevailing rates. Emergency liquidations of flocks may be required, for example—estate settlements ("He left us his *what?!*"), divorce cases ("Who gets custody of the chickens?"), and unanticipated landscaping alterations ("They ate my pelargoniums!"). If you follow the classified ads and feed store bulletin boards and are willing to wait, you may find what you want for almost any price, maybe even for free. But be on the alert, especially when a supposed bargain is in the offing. Following the used-car buyers' philosophy, try to bring along a friend who knows his chickens so he can help confirm your judgment.

SOURCES

Sources for eggs, chicks, and mature chickens are private parties, found through classified ads, county fair exhibits, or poultry clubs and their newsletters; farm catalogs (Sears, Wards, Nasco, etc.); poultry mail-order firms; hatcheries; and sometimes feed stores. All sources won't necessarily sell all three. Some specialize in selling hatching eggs, some in young chicks, and some won't sell a bird until it's fully feathered. Each has a good reason: selling only eggs frees the seller from the bother of hatching. Selling chicks means the seller won't have to raise them. Selling mature chickens ensures that the seller won't have customers complaining because they got too many cockerels or because the chickens didn't turn out exactly as expected; it also gives the seller a chance to take his pick of the flock for next year's breeding.

Whenever possible, we like to purchase stock locally instead of through the mail. You can see not only the parent stock and the stock you are about to acquire but also the conditions under which they have been raised. You also can determine whether or not they are healthy. The birds will be used to the local climate and won't have as difficult a time adjusting to the move as birds that are shipped. You will have the added advantage of being able to go back to the breeder if you have any questions or problems. Nevertheless, if you hear of a place from which you would like to order by mail, try to find out about the place

143

first. See if you can find someone else who has ordered from them and ask if they were satisfied with what they got. Sometimes you order what you want and the company sends you what *they* want. Often their "breeds" are of questionable authenticity. Make sure they guarantee live delivery. Specify whether you want show or pet quality, and be prepared to pay a higher price for the former.

You can also purchase eggs through the mail from a number of places, but again we recommend purchasing locally when possible, as you can then examine the parent stock for vigor and see that they are the kind of chickens you would like to have. You can pick out eggs that conform to the requirements for good hatchability that we described in Chapter 9, "The Setting Hen." Don't be afraid to be choosey when you purchase hatching eggs. There's no point in wasting time and money on eggs that might not hatch. If you buy your eggs in person, you will also avoid the possibility that the eggs have been mishandled in transit. When purchasing eggs far from home, pad them well for the long ride so that they won't get too jostled. Scrambled eggs won't hatch. We knew one woman who would pick up her eggs one by one and shake them, saying, "I wonder if *this* one will hatch." Probably not.

SUMMARY

Here, briefly stated, are the primary considerations in starting a flock.

- Take time and care in choosing your breeds. Look through the *Standard of Perfection,* and pick a breed that's aesthetically pleasing to you and whose characteristics suit your purposes.
- Start with enough birds to get the flock going but not so many that the available space is overcrowded. For many backyard flocks, a trio (one cock and two hens) is an excellent beginning.
- Whether you start with eggs, chicks, or chickens depends largely on how much time and money you are willing to spend on your birds initially.
- There are many factors involved in the selling price of a chicken. By doing a little shopping first, you will learn to tell if a given bird is a bargain, overpriced, or just about right.
- Where you purchase your first birds will to a large extent be determined by what breed or breeds you decide to raise. Make an attempt to choose a reputable source nearby so that you can be assured of a happy experience with your first flock.

16
Chickens for Fun

We don't have a television. We don't need one. Our need for passive entertainment is satisfied by a show that doesn't use electricity or cause a radiation hazard. Best of all, it's never interrupted by commercials! We simply climb into our cherry tree armchair and instantly become absorbed in the intrigues of barnyard society. There's only one channel, it's true, but the programming is live, in color, and endlessly varied: we can referee crowing contests, watch a hen proudly parade her newly hatched chicks around, or root for the little guy in a soccer game involving a freshly found worm. It's a marvelous excuse to put off mowing the lawn or doing the dishes. Sometimes we run out to get the eggs for breakfast and don't get back till lunchtime.

The din in the barnyard creates the illusion that the world of people is far away. The general bustle of crowing, clucking, cackling, and squawking makes it nearly impossible to hear someone calling from the house. A name shouted across the yard may sound like just another of the many variations of a rooster's crow. We finally installed a loud gong: one bang means "soup's on," two bangs mean "company's here," three bangs mean "telephone call." (More than three means a visitor's child has discovered the gong and a new way to amuse himself.)

Spending time with the flock and getting to know the chickens is made all the more charming by the fact that each bird has its own personality. Some are aggressive, having an opinion on every subject; others are unassuming, the type you hardly notice; one now and then is inquisitive, quite oblivious to the hazards of hanging around the business end of an operating garden tool; some talk all the time, muttering away to no

146

one in particular the whole day long as they make their rounds, and no one in particular paying them a bit of attention. The roosters' crows are distinctive enough that the owner can easily identify each bird—even from under the covers at the break of dawn. People who don't raise chickens are amazed when the owner of a flock can point out each chicken and mention some distinguishing characteristic by which he identifies the bird. To the uninitiated they're all alike.

Observing the fantastic variety of subtle social interactions among chickens has given us insight into birds in general. We find that many of the social customs of chickens apply to wild birds as well. Now when we see birds courting on the front lawn, their peculiar antics are not so mysterious to us.

Your friends will think you're crazy if you try to tell them how interesting chickens are. But once they find out, they'll likely be hooked, too. It might even do something dramatic to them. We have a young friend who was hired to help an elderly man care for his flock. He found the experience so fascinating that he changed his college major to avian science.

There are plenty of good things about raising chickens— fresh eggs, delicious meat, bug and weed control, a continuous supply of fertilizer for the garden, prizes at the fair—but you really don't need a reason. Raising chickens is just plain fun!

Appendix

PUBLICATIONS

The Avian Embryo, #MM-207, Cooperative Extension Service, Ohio State University, Columbus, Ohio 43210. A good description of what goes on within a hatching egg; includes a description of building a small incubator.

Bantam Standard, and quarterly bantam culture course lessons, American Bantam Association, Box 464, Chicago, Illinois 60690. This book is similar to the APA *Standard* but deals with bantam chickens only.

Diseases of Poultry, H. E. Biester and L. H. Schwarte, editors, the Iowa State University Press, Ames, Iowa 50010. This is the standard reference work that vets often use. It is complete and authoritative, but it is expensive and many amateurs find it too technical.

From Egg to Chick, circular #878, College of Agriculture, University of Illinois, Urbana, Illinois 61801. Contains instructions for building an incubator and hatching in it.

A Manual of Poultry Diseases, Texas Agricultural Extension Service, Texas A & M University, College Station, Texas 77844. An inexpensive guide to poultry diseases and their prevention.

The Merck Veterinary Manual, A Handbook of Diagnosis and Therapy for the Veterinarian, Merck & Co., Inc., Rahway, New Jersey 07065, 1973. This handy veterinary guide contains information not only on poultry diseases but also on problems of other farm animals.

Poultry Press, Box 947, York, Pennsylvania 17405. This monthly newspaper contains news of poultry shows throughout the country and sometimes gives helpful tips on bird care.

Raising Poultry the Modern Way, Leonard S. Mercia, Garden Way Publishers, Charlotte, Vermont 05445, 1974. Deals basically with commercial methods of maintaining fairly small ranch flocks.

149

Salsbury Manual of Poultry Diseases, Salsbury Laboratory, Charles City, Iowa 50616. This is a very inexpensive, clearly written publication on poultry diseases.

Selecting, Fitting, and Showing Poultry, Julius E. Nordby, The Interstate Printers and Publishers, Inc., Danville, Illinois 61832. Now out of print, this is one of the few books on preparing poultry for show.

Standard of Perfection, American Poultry Association, 26363 South Tucker Road, Estacada, Oregon 97023. A must for those interested in showing poultry, and fun to look at for everyone else. It gives the standards by which each variety is judged and includes pictures of most breeds.

FURTHER INFORMATION

Information Division, USDA, Washington, D.C. 20205. Free publications and advice; *Home Canning of Meat and Poultry,* Home and Garden bulletin #106; *Home Freezing of Poultry,* Home and Garden bulletin #70.

Superintendent of Public Documents, Government Printing Office, Washington, D.C. 20204. *Caponizing Chickens,* publication #490. (Also ask for list of publications. They are not free but are inexpensive.)

Agricultural Extension Service or Cooperative Extension Service, United States Department of Agriculture. A local source of free pamphlets and advice. (Look in the phone book under your county government.)

Feed stores. Free pamphlets provided by feed companies, usually geared for commercial farms, but of some use to backyard husbanders.

EQUIPMENT AND SUPPLIES

Brower Manufacturing Company, 640 South Fifth Street, Quincy, Illinois 62301. Manufacturer of poultry equipment including incubators, feeders and waterers, and water heating devices.

Havahart, Box 551, Ossining, New York 10562. Sells traps that will not harm the caught animal.

150

Lyon Electric Company, PO Box 81303, San Diego, California 92138. Sells electrical poultry equipment including incubators, brooders, water-pipe heater tapes, and hard to find incubator parts for building and repairing home units.

Marsh Manufacturing Inc., 14232 Brookhurst Street, Garden Grove, California 92643. Catalog lists a large assortment of bird related books, small incubators and brooders, catching nets, and other supplies.

Nasco, Fort Atkinson, Wisconsin 53538 *or* 1524 Princeton Avenue, Modesto, California 95352. Farm and ranch supplies.

Robbins Incubator Company, PO Box 899, Denver, Colorado 80201. Manufacturer of commercial incubators for large hatcheries, but sells one smaller model (180-egg) that has all of the features of the larger automatic commercial types.

Rocky Top Poultry Supplies, PO Box 1006, Harriman, Tennessee 37748. Lists a wide assortment of books, cages, automatic watering devices, incubators, and so forth.

Sears, Roebuck Company and Montgomery Ward. Farm catalogs may be ordered through your local catalog sales office.

Stromberg's, 50 Lake Route, Pine River, Minnesota 56474. A fascinating catalog of stock, equipment, and books.

(Also check with local hatcheries and feed stores.)

Index